Persistent Poverty

Persistent Poverty

Voices from the Margins

Jamie Swift, Brice Balmer, and Mira Dineen

Between the Lines
Toronto

Persistent Poverty: Voices from the Margins

© 2010 by Jamie Swift, Brice Balmer, and Mira Dineen

First published in Canada in 2010 by
Between the Lines
401 Richmond Street West, Studio 277
Toronto, Ontario
M5V 3A8

1-800-718-7201

www.btlbooks.com

Library and Archives Canada Cataloguing in Publication
Swift, Jamie, 1951–
        Persistent poverty : voices from the margins / Jamie Swift, Brice Balmer and Mira Dineen.
Interfaith Social Assistance Reform Coalition's 2010 social audit report.
ISBN 978-1-897071-73-1

1. Poor – Ontario – Social conditions. 2. Poverty – Government policy – Ontario.
3. Public welfare – Ontario. 4. Ontario – Social conditions. I. Balmer, Brice H.,
1944– II. Dineen, Mira III. Interfaith Social Assistance Reform Coalition IV. Title.
HC120.P6S95 2010   362.509713   C2010-906209-4

Cover design and front cover photo by Jennifer Tiberio
Text design and page preparation by Steve Izma
Printed in Canada
Second Printing March 2011

MIX
Paper from
responsible sources
FSC® C004071

Between the Lines gratefully acknowledges assistance for its publishing activities from the Canada Council for the Arts, the Ontario Arts Council, the Government of Ontario through the Ontario Book Publishers Tax Credit program and through the Ontario Book Initiative, and the Government of Canada through the Canada Book Fund.

 Canada Council   Conseil des Arts
for the Arts   du Canada

 Canadä

 ONTARIO ARTS COUNCIL
CONSEIL DES ARTS DE L'ONTARIO

Contents

Introduction:
The Work of Hundreds of People

"**P**ERSISTENT POVERTY." Our book's title points to the enduring plight of our most vulnerable neighbours. Its subtitle, "Voices from the Margins," describes what the book offers: an opportunity for people whose voices are too rarely heard to describe life on the precarious edge of a culture that tends to place more value on celebrity than on human dignity.

This kind of survey is becoming more urgent. In 2010 the federal Conservative government decided to abandon the census techniques that had long provided detailed and reliable data about poverty in our rich country. From the ruling government's point of view, the less we know about the poor, the easier it is to overlook them. A recent headline says it all: "Poverty Increases Chances of Dying of Cancer, Study Says."[1] The study in question was based on the long-form census data that Ottawa would eliminate. Political moves like this make the need for this book all the more pressing.

The book has three authors, but the organizing, writing, consulting, testifying, and facilitating that stand behind it involved a great many more people scattered across Ontario. The Interfaith Social Assistance Reform Coalition (ISARC) 2010 social audit process engaged several hundred volunteers who organized hearings across the province. These volunteers, working as convenors, facilitators, recorders, and rapporteurs, heard from several thousand people who described the effects of poverty in their lives and communities.[2] We hope that these voices, which animate the following pages, will be heard not just by the political class but also, indeed, by all Ontario residents.

ISARC's roots go back to the Ontario Social Assistance Review Committee, established in 1986. This official government inquiry held hearings in thirteen communities and produced *Transitions* (1988), a report that captured the voices of low-income Ontarians. That document was, unfortunately, shelved. ISARC later held thirteen community hearings of its own in the course of audits done in 1991, 1998, and 2003. Reports based on those audits went to all members of the Ontario legislature and were used by faith groups, teachers, social justice groups, and activists. The 2010 audit doubled to twenty-six the number of communities in which we held hearings.

The 2010 social audit includes for the first time too a significant rural component – an important addition given the vast impact of poverty throughout Ontario, and not just in urban centres. In this regard Aboriginal and Northern peoples should certainly have been included in the audit, but unfortunately ISARC did not have the finances, contacts, and staff time to publicize and co-ordinate our work among these peoples. This remains a serious gap.

In the end ISARC's social audit was a qualitative process in which the authors and local reporters pulled together elements of testimonies by topics and categories. The resulting stories spoke their own truths. We asked people about their experiences of poverty, about whether poverty had changed in the last five years, and how they might break the cycle of poverty individually and as a community. We deeply appreciate the courage of the low-income people who brought their experiences to the hearings. Because of the stigma that they face, their participation is all the more appreciated.

□

ISARC has advocated for government social audits for the past fifteen years, and when it was in opposition the provincial Liberal Party put forward a bill to establish a social audit. Still, "social audit" is not common parlance. Perhaps in another five years time we will find a different term to apply to these hearings. Most people, though, are familiar with the idea of fiscal and environmental audits. A social audit seeks to determine the social and community consequences of acts of legislation or of changing rules and regulations. Does the legislation yield the expected results? Are there other consequences?

For instance, when the Ontario government reduced workplace inspectors in the mid-1990s, deaths and accidents increased significantly, with a deep and lasting impact on the lives of countless people and families. When labour standards inspections declined, employer violations of laws governing hard-won labour rights around overtime and working hours increased. Drastic reductions in social assistance and affordable housing increased homelessness in Ontario. With these reductions, food banks found that 6 to 10 per cent of their patrons had *no* income – a new phenomenon. When the minimum wage was increased and the Ontario Child Benefit was implemented, the results were improved incomes for many families and a reduction of child poverty in Ontario.

Over the past five years an Ontario movement for poverty elimination has been steadily growing, partly thanks to the work of the Social Planning Network of Ontario, the 25 in 5 Network for Poverty Reduction, Campaign 2000, the Income Security Advocacy Centre, the Ontario Coalition Against Poverty, and many other groups. People who provide survival and charity services asked politicians and governments when poverty would be eliminated. The provincial government responded with minimum-wage increases, an Ontario Child Benefit, the Ontario Poverty Reduction Strategy, the Ontario *Poverty Reduction Act*, and a Social Assistance Review Advisory Committee report.

Yet the pace of change has been discouragingly slow. The 2010 provincial budget's support for poverty elimination was minimal at best. The budget promised to scrap the Special Diet Allowance (SDA), but provided no details on a Nutritious Food Allowance. Elimination of the Special Diet Allowance created significant angst among Ontario Works (OW) and Ontario Disability Support Program (ODSP) recipients, who already lack the resources to pay the rent and purchase sufficient food. The government also delayed the Affordable Housing Strategy and did not move to eliminate the "stupid rules" that make the lives of OW and ODSP recipients so difficult.

Back in 1998 the atmosphere in Ontario had been so poisoned by poor-bashing and punitive attitudes that many people were afraid to speak up at public hearings. In 2003 ISARC decided that all future audits would use the "United Nations Human Rapporteur" model.[3] This is a model used in oppressive countries, with hearings generally held only in places in which people are accustomed to gather. The news media are not invited; governments are not notified. UN rapporteurs listen to participants' words and submit written reports. The process ensures safety, confidentiality, and truthfulness.

Thankfully, fear was not as evident in the 2010 ISARC social audit as it was in 1998 and 2003. People clearly felt more comfortable speaking, and tended to be more engaged, when they knew who was in the room and were reassured that confidentiality would be maintained throughout the process.

Will Ontario's momentum for poverty elimination continue to increase? Will we stand in solidarity with those who suffer because of low incomes, inadequate housing, lack of opportunities, hunger, and stigmatization? Will we create communities where human dignity holds pride of place? It is up to each of us – and all of us together – to address, and answer, these questions.

1 "As Sharp As You Could Cut Them"

I really appreciate the opportunity to be part of the audit. I have been trying to make sure that what is going on with me is able to help, somehow. . . . At the very least I am able to tell my story.
— Marie, social assistance recipient, Halton

O N A GREY AUTUMN DAY in 1995 a group of women lined up in front of Kingston's City Hall. A newly elected provincial government was declaring that the province's programs to provide affordable housing to the poor were a "boondoggle." The Catholic Sisters did not agree. They disagreed more when the government proceeded to abandon social housing.

In Kingston, a small city at the northeast corner of Lake Ontario, the social divisions are, in the words of Robertson Davies, "as sharp as you could cut them." The eminent novelist's family had long been the owner of the local newspaper. Another eminent Ontario intellectual and long-time Kingstonian, historian Arthur Lower, described the isolation of Kingston's poor in a north-end ghetto as "segregation."[1]

The women who assembled at lunchtime in 1995 were well aware of the plight of the city's marginalized people. They were heir to a tradition of giving aid to their most vulnerable neighbours – a tradition stretching back to 1865, when the Sisters of Providence of St. Vincent de Paul first set about working on behalf of the orphaned, the sick, and the aged. The Sisters embarked on exhausting and humbling "begging tours" to the town's wealthier districts, seeking money to shelter and feed those in their care. By 1995 their mission had gone beyond charity. The Sisters had committed themselves to promoting "structures and relationships of equality and mutuality through attitudes and actions for justice and peace."

At the time the Progressive Conservative government under Mike Harris had begun cutting social assistance rates and indulging in a rampant round of poor-bashing. With an eye on marketing but with no apparent sense of irony, the government would call its niggardly welfare system "Ontario Works." The Sisters could not stand for this, so they decided to stand up against it.

Some fifteen years later the Sisters and their little band of supporters were still standing on what had become a familiar strip of sidewalk. Tourists alighting from buses and locals lunching in nearby Confederation Park and driving along Ontario Street could not help but notice the signs. *Housing Not War. Poverty Doesn't Take a Holiday* (emblazoned with palms tree and a sunny beach). *Make Poverty History.* One little sign featured the word *Greed* with a red slash through it.

Jean Chrétien had been elected prime minister not long before the Sisters started their vigil. Since then they have stood against the invasion of Iraq and for the preservation of Kingston's prison farms. But their main focus has remained the plight of far too many poor people in a province with such vast riches. They have been on the sidewalk every Friday in all kinds of weather – with as few as three participants and as many as four hundred at a tenth anniversary gathering when vigil supporters wrapped City Hall in a 400-metre white banner. Two Sisters, both in their eighties, stitched together the banner from discarded hospital sheets.

The vigil keepers have a little handout for passers-by. It includes a brief interfaith prayer and a challenge: "How would you feel if your income had declined by 41 per cent during the past 15 years? This has happened to our neighbours on social assistance." Despite dozens of trips to Queen's Park for lobbying meetings organized by Ontario's faith-based social justice group ISARC (Interfaith Social Assistance Reform Coalition), and despite a long string of polite meetings with their MPP – an influential cabinet minister in the Liberal government that took office in 2003 – they have received no satisfactory answer to this question. So they have continued to stand, as their little pamphlet says, "in silent, non-violent solidarity with those affected by government and corporations that put profits before humankind and indeed before all Creation."

□

The Kingston Sisters have been long-time supporters of ISARC. The faith communities that came together to form the organization share the vision outlined in 1988 by Ontario's official Social Assistance Review Committee – a vision of a society "based on fairness, shared responsibility and personal dignity for all." But they realized that if those words were to lead to action, voices of conscience would need to get to the very roots of the problem. To speak truth to power, ISARC believed, Ontario's political leaders had to listen to the voices of those most harmed by decisions ostensibly being made to relieve their suffering.

In the twenty-one years that followed, ISARC convened four sets of community consultations that came to be known as "social audits." These consultations sought above all else to give voice to the voiceless. The 1990 *Neighbour to Neighbour: Voices for Change* report outlined the lack of progress being made as Ontario headed into what was then the most severe downturn since the Great Depression of the 1930s. In 1997 ISARC organized a second set of community soundings just as the punitive reforms that brought in Ontario Works (OW) and the Ontario Disability Support Program (ODSP) began making their mark. Having listened to the victims' voices, ISARC concluded that the new system made low-income people feel "distrusted and despised."

Out of those 1997 hearings came ISARC's 1998 report, *Our Neighbours' Voices: Will We Listen?* Unfortunately, dozens of the stories in that report bear a sobering similarity to accounts in the pages that follow. One woman, Joanne, outlined her experiences with a social assistance system that she said was "based on distrust more than anything else." At a time when the Employment Insurance system covered far more workers than it does today, Joanne could not get benefits because her work had been short-term. When the welfare system was reformed, "the endless fear and worry and anger began." She became stressed out and unmotivated. Her performance at her volunteer job declined. She noticed that she was no longer as well organized as she used to be. She found herself learning at a slower rate. When her doctor suggested antidepressants, Joanne said she wanted to be left alone to run her own life. The welfare workers assumed she was a cheat. "It feels like being a criminal," she told us. "You have no financial privacy at all."[2]

Later, on the eve of a provincial election, ISARC launched its third set of public consultations on poverty. Based on a United Nations rapporteur model of special listeners hearing the testimonies of low-income people, the 2003 social audit once again sought out those most hurt by Ontario's deepening crisis of poverty and hunger. ISARC's hearings in thirteen centres were aimed at enabling as many of our fellow citizens as possible to understand the needs of strangers, what it is like to fall on hard times and be forced to seek help from public providers and private charities. The stories in our report *Lives in the Balance* struck what were by then familiar chords: stigma, fear, poverty-level wages, humiliation, low self-esteem. Yet the final chapter – "Ontario at a Turning Point" – of the first edition struck a hopeful note because with the upcoming election we sensed a possible shift in the political wind. Indeed, with that election of 2003 the rule of the Progressive Conservatives and their so-called Common Sense Revolution came to an end. A Liberal government took power.

It would be another seven years before we organized our next social audit. In the interim ISARC became part of a broad-based effort that gave rise to the 25 in 5 Network for Poverty Reduction in Ontario. During the lead-up to the 2007 election, we published a second edition of our 2003 report. Its title, *Lives Still in the Balance*, hinted strongly that conditions for Ontario's low-income people had changed very little since the first edition was published. We outlined the government's "tentative baby steps" in the direction of a socially just and inclusive community.

ISARC welcomed the introduction of the newly elected government's *Poverty Reduction Act* and the remarkable all-party consensus that led to its unanimous adoption in 2009. Another hopeful sign was an Ontario Poverty Reduction Strategy that had earlier committed the province to reducing the number of children living in poverty by 25 per cent over five years. The government also increased the Ontario Child Benefit to $1,100 per child per year. Yet optimism was tempered by the caveat – some called it political wiggle room – that the government inserted as a "quick fact" in announcing the passage of the Act: "Meeting the 25 in 5 target will require provincial investments, federal investments and a growing economy."[3]

The reference to federal investments translates into the tendency, common in Canada's federal system, for governments at one level to point fingers at and pass bucks to another level. It was with such caveats in mind – and being equally mindful of how taxing and spending priorities really define any government – that ISARC organized its first ever prayer vigil at Queen's Park. During three chilly weeks leading up to Ontario's March 2009 budget, a leader of one of ISARC's participating faith communities led a daily interfaith prayer service. The vigil keepers were praying that Ontario's politicians would have the strength of character and courage to do the right thing.

"Certainly, we have democracy, free economy, the ability to earn," said Rabbi Tina Grimberg. "But our inability to sustain those in need is a *bushah* – in Hebrew this means a shame. . . . A roof over one's head is not a privilege, it's a right."

Reflecting on the meaning and potential of the pre-budget vigil, the Rabbi added: "How can it not have an effect if there are dedicated, caring people praying in a loving way, asking that the [plight] of our most vulnerable in society be brought up to our lawmakers. . . . We don't know how many people we touch when we do goodness in this world. I refuse to believe that we don't do good here. This is a *mitzvah*."[4] A mitzvah is a commandment or good deed.

In the end the government's 2009 budget was a disappointment. The government increased the Ontario Child Benefit and minimum wage but implemented only a marginal increase in social assistance. Affordable housing monies were far less than anticipated. ISARC thus decided that it was time once again to take the pulse of the province by organizing our fourth – and most extensive – series of public soundings, talking to low-income people in twenty-six different communities. The hearings took place across Southern Ontario, with a few meetings in the North. Listeners included civic and religious leaders who acted as "rapporteurs." Many of those leaders had not heard the stories of people on low incomes.

□

Gambling has deep roots in our culture. The Ontario government profits massively from what it prefers to call "gaming," while many non-profit groups depend on bingo revenues for their survival. Bingo parlours dot low-income communities across the province, rivalling food banks and meal programs in number and attracting people longing to "get lucky." But luck is important in all our lives. In the following pages you will read about only a small fraction of the people whom we encountered between February and June of 2010. Particularly striking was just how often *simple bad luck* figured in the plight of those who so generously gave their time to us.

One ISARC volunteer, reflecting on what she had heard in the tiny southeastern Ontario village of Mountain, reflected on how we see our marginalized neighbours, the stigma, the shame . . . and the bad luck: "Before we judge too harshly we might remember that it might be any of us if life takes a different twist of fate. I wonder how each of us would handle having our choices taken away, the need to swallow our pride, vulnerability worn on our sleeves for all to see, the need to wear our neighbours' shoes and coats, and to have our voices no longer heard. I wonder how we would feel when we hear someone asking why we have a dog and cat when we do not have enough money to feed ourselves. Little do they realize that our pet is the only one that does not judge us, and loves us and sits with us when we cry because we are alone?"

A simple twist of fate – this is the reality that underpins so many of the stories we heard.

Agnes and her husband had four children when she found him dead in the basement, killed by his own hand. After she learned of the suicide clause in their insurance policy – which meant no insurance benefits for herself and her children – she went on the program then called Mother's Allowance before later remarrying. Some twelve years and two more children later, that marriage dissolved when her husband became abusive. She had recently returned to school to obtain certification as a personal support worker. Also qualified in early childhood education, she was now the prototypical working-class woman in service-sector employment – in Agnes's case the low-paid end of the "caring professions."

As she got older, Agnes found it increasingly difficult to cope with the long shifts in which she looked after other people's needs. Diagnosed with chronic obstructive pulmonary disease, she kept on working until her children were on their own, although money was always tight. Life is particularly difficult for low-income people who are single, so she moved in first with her sister and then with a married couple she knew. She had to move when that marriage broke up. When she spoke to ISARC volunteers at the Halton social audit, she was sleeping on her son's couch. She was adamant that her children were all very good to her, but explained that what she really craved was privacy. She found it hard, this couch-surfing, having to ask if she can have a shower or get something from the fridge.

"All of my stuff is in my daughter's garage," she said, adding that it was hard to get social assistance without a fixed address. "The clothes I wear, I keep in the trunk of my car. I tell my son I'm going out to my closet."

Agnes's wry humour could not mask her feelings about the hard hand she had been dealt. "I'm sad because I am not in this position because I want to be. . . . I feel like I'm in a hole and I can't get out. I don't want to be rich. I don't want anything that doesn't belong to me."

She said that one bit of good luck is that she had a wonderful family doctor. "If it wasn't for him, I'd probably be in a straitjacket." Unfortunately, at Christmas 2009 her doctor told her about a tumour on her lung.

Needless to say, the stories we heard were far from cheery. But they did provide important insights into how our affluent society works.

A Welland social justice advocate pointed out that many people fail to realize that all it takes is a sudden, debilitating job loss or illness and you can find yourself in the same situation as those whom you once saw as "those people."

A low-income person in Simcoe County described the stigma that gnawed at her. "People look at you differently. They watch what you buy at a grocery store. People know you are poor."

A woman in North Bay focused on the fear that poor people experience when they deal with the authorities. "I know a woman who was so anxious and fearful about losing money that she didn't even visit her hospitalized partner." The woman she was speaking of was afraid that the social assistance officers would find out that she and her partner had been living together, which raises a red flag in the eyes of the system.

A North Bay service provider explained recent changes in her clientele. "I'm seeing a new group of working poor who have done everything the right way and are now in need. They were the 'haves' but are now the 'have-nots.' They are harder to service as they cannot get instant service and resent the kinds of detailed questions we need to ask about the financial situation and history. They have an expectation of privacy. They didn't realize that getting help would be so intrusive. They simply cannot figure out what they have done wrong."

These are the people, she said, who believe they should be somehow treated differently. They say, "But I'm not like the other people you deal with."

□

The new group of working poor underlines a troubling trend that has been steadily emerging since ISARC's first community probe into poverty in 1990. That was when Ontario was just beginning to be ravaged by a major recession. As with any downturn, there was a spike in poverty as people lost jobs. The recession that hit in 2008 also resulted in increased hardship, made even more difficult because there are now fewer government supports in place. In the meantime personal debt has increased and savings have plummeted even though people are working longer hours. By 2009 only 41 per cent of unemployed Ontario workers were collecting Employment Insurance benefits.[5] Moreover, many of the Ontario jobs created in the economic boom that lasted from 1997 to 2007 paid less than $10 an hour.[6] Coupled with the long-term trend to a split-level job market divided between precarious (part-time, contract, temporary) jobs and full-time work with benefits, this trend has dire implications for working-class people and indeed for society at large.

When it comes to discussions of Ontario's stubbornly and shamefully high poverty levels, there is an elephant in the room: inequality – the highly skewed way in which wealth is distributed. In the period since faith communities got together to form ISARC in 1986, the overall size of the economic pie has roughly doubled. Collectively, we produce twice as much in the way of goods and services as we did a generation ago. But the pie is becoming ever more unequally divided. In 2008 a Statistics Canada report remarked on the "sharp growth" of earnings among the rich. It also showed that, in Ontario, the percentage of jobs paying under $10 an hour had actually risen during the 1997–2007 job boom, when unemployment fell dramatically. The rising tide of economic growth has clearly not lifted all boats. The average earnings of Ontario managers grew by 19 per cent in this period. As a Statistics Canada report put it, "In contrast, blue collar workers in manufacturing, clerical employees and salespersons in retails trade experienced virtually no earnings growth."[7]

Put another way, in 1976 the earnings of the richest 10 per cent of Ontario families were twenty-seven times those of the poorest families. A generation later, by 2004, the richest 10 per cent enjoyed earnings seventy-five times those of the poorest.[8] In more time-tested parlance, the rich are getting richer, the poor poorer. This sad trend points to a material success that is accompanied by social failure.

From a faith perspective the stark numbers and the testimony that we heard in the spring of 2010 are ethically disturbing, to say the least. Human dignity is inherent in each of us. We are not valuable only because we are consumers or producers. Human dignity is based not on economic status, but on equity of opportunity. We must all be seen as being valuable to the communities we live in, large or small – faith groups, neighbourhoods, or cities. Everyone has a contribution to make. Rather than operating on the basis of stigma, faith communities are guided by compassion and justice, and especially by the idea of walking with others who face apparently intractable problems of poverty. Persistent poverty is especially offensive to those stalwarts in the faith communities who provide food, shelter, and other essentials to low-income people.

The dilemma is not just a matter of the poor dying younger or suffering disproportionately from preventable disease. Nor is it simply the basic injustice of a province that has a superabundance of unshared bread. It is also about social *exclusion*. Marketers know how effective it is to suggest that we can set ourselves apart from others by having certain things. That is why they use the word "exclusive." In the audit it was common for us to hear the stories of mothers – stressed and depressed as they tried to provide even the most basic food and shelter – who remarked on how hurtful it was when their children came to them asking if they could go on a school trip with the other kids or have a pair of shoes like the other kids.

Long after Kingston's Sisters of Providence started their silent vigil, another exclusive private school opened in a former soft-drink bottling plant in town. The school's compulsory tartan and blazer uniforms cost hundreds of dollars, but that expense is dwarfed by the exclusive King's Town School's annual fees, *$8,360 to send a child to Grade 1.* A single adult on social assistance *receives $7,020 each year.*

It is against this background of savage inequality in a fabulously wealthy province that the Sisters of Providence have continued their fifteen-year vigil in front of City Hall, handing out the little pamphlet that asks, "Why is it necessary for Kingston's faith communities to provide nearly 8,000 meals every month to people who are hungry?" They are convinced that far, far too little has changed despite the actions of a provincial government that – despite small improvements in addressing social justice – is seemingly content to live with the continuing humiliation of the poor.

The last week of every month finds Sister Peggy Flanagan, seventy-two, at the Salvation Army "Bread of Life" meal program. By that time, money has run out and cupboards are bare in the north-end neighbourhood served by the program in which Sister Peggy peels carrots and dishes up hot meals. Some people may have appealed to the local food bank as a stopgap, but you can only do that once a month. As she stands at City Hall holding a *Know Peace, Know Justice* sign, Sister Peggy has often been heard to paraphrase St. Vincent de Paul: "When you feed the poor, please ask for their forgiveness. You are giving them a bowl of soup but they give up their dignity."

2 Back to the Future?
The Choice Is Ours

Armine Yalnizyan, with Jamie Swift

> The poor of Canada, the dispossessed, are largely an invisible problem. They are with us but not of us. We don't come in contact with them. We know they exist and most of us believe something should be done about it, but that's about all.
>
> – Senator David Croll, 1972

S ENATOR DAVID CROLL WAS BORN in a Russian *shtetl* in 1900 and arrived in Windsor, Ontario, with his parents when he was eight. He rose from shoeshine boy to Liberal lawyer before becoming Windsor's mayor in the middle of the Great Depression (1931–34), Ontario's first Jewish cabinet minister (1934–37), a federal MP by 1945, and Canada's first Jewish Senator in 1955. By 1972, when he made a wonderfully conversational speech to the well-heeled and influential audience of the Empire Club in Toronto, he had guided the preparation of two landmark Senate reports: one on aging (1966), and the other on poverty (1971).[1]

The Senator's report on aging provided a crucial boost to Canada's fledgling efforts to cut poverty among its elderly population. The 1960s and early 1970s saw the introduction and development of a raft of public provisions, such as the Canada and Quebec pension plans, the old age supplement, and the guaranteed income supplements. Together these government programs succeeded in consistently and dramatically reducing poverty *and* inequality, particularly among senior citizens. In the mid-1970s the poverty rate for seniors was close to 30 per cent, with elderly women suffering rates of almost 35 per cent.[2] Today it is around 5 per cent.

Senator Croll died in 1991. Still a sitting Senator in 1989, he no doubt experienced mixed emotions when the House of Commons passed its unanimous resolution to end child poverty by 2000. But it is hard to imagine him being anything but disheartened by the facts of poverty today, and by where most elected officials stand on the issue.

His words about the invisibility of the poor and the passivity of the rest of us could, tragically, have been spoken yesterday. Indeed, they were.

In 2010 musician and writer Dave Bidini wrote in the *National Post*, perhaps the national newspaper that most regularly displays a dim view of the poor in our midst: "When you live in a big city, homeless people start to become like pigeons. . . . Because they're so ubiquitous, they seem part of the city's wallpaper, which the citizenry largely moves past, rarely pausing to consider how near we are to their condition."[3]

□

Much has changed since Senator Croll's 1971 report on poverty, but much remains the same.

Other nations, notably those in Northern Europe and Scandinavia, have in the intervening years tackled and almost eliminated rates of poverty among seniors, working-age adults, and young families. Canada has had success with seniors, but largely ignored the plight of the disabled, unemployed, working poor, Aboriginal peoples, and children – and this is not for want of economic success. Poverty among children leaves the longest legacy and saps the future potential of societies and economies alike. And it is among children that it becomes devastatingly clear that fighting poverty requires more than strong labour markets alone. The variation in child poverty rates among upper-income nations is testament to that fact. Over time child poverty rates have fallen to less than 5 per cent in Denmark, Finland, Norway, and Sweden. Child poverty was slightly higher in Germany, the Netherlands, and Switzerland (between 6 and 9 per cent); and an even higher proportion of children lived in poverty in Australia, the United Kingdom, Israel, and Poland (between 11 and 20 per cent). In the United States, a staggering 22 per cent of children lived in poor families before the global economic crisis unfolded. In Canada, child poverty rates did not dip below double digit rates until 2007, but the recession promises to undo that slow and wholly inadequate decline in child poverty.[4]

Our society has been transformed by galloping economic growth, particularly in the decade preceding the global economic meltdown that started in 2008. From 1990 to 2008, the value of the Canadian economy more than doubled (from $680 billion to $1.6 trillion), and the nation's net worth tripled (from just over $2 trillion to just over $6 trillion). If the way to solve poverty is by growing the economic pie, we should have supplied all the pieces we need to solve *that* particular problem long ago.

The problem of poverty is not simply about the size of the economic pie, and how big you can grow it, but how it is divvied up. The most recent decade of blockbuster growth, unparalleled by anything since the 1960s, is categorically different from that earlier decade in the way in which the money was distributed and used. Back in the 1960s, even though poverty was still a major problem, a strong economy translated to widespread prosperity, not just in the form of rising paycheques for the vast majority, but in the form of growing access to a wide range of public goods, from income supports to parks, rinks, libraries, better schools, more universities, and state-of-the-art hospitals.

Canada's most recent burst of economic growth has been accompanied by stubbornly high rates of poverty among working-age adults, decaying public infrastructure, and staggering amounts of cheap stuff. There have been jaw-dropping increases in pay for some, but the majority has watched pay rates and working conditions stay the same or decline. Incomes have risen for those at the bottom, to be sure; but that is because more people now have jobs than did people in the mid-1990s, and more people are working longer hours. For those at the top – people who are putting in the same work effort as measured by time and have the same smarts as measured by credentials – somehow the value of their work has shot through the roof.

Our top one hundred CEOs took in, on average, $7.3 million each in 2008. The average worker made $42,000 that year. In 1998 the average compensation of Canada's top one hundred CEOs was $3.5 million, while the average worker made $40,000. Take inflation into account, and the pay packets of the top guns have outpaced price increases by 70 per cent while average workers have lost ground: the purchasing power of their income has fallen by 6 per cent, with any gains more than eaten up by rising costs.[5]

In 2008 the pay packet of an average CEO in the top one hundred was equal to 174 average workers. In 1998 he (and they are all males) was worth 110 average workers. Are the captains of industry really worth so much more to their companies and to the Canadian economy today than they were a decade ago? To put it another way, is the average Canadian worker really worth so much less?

The contrast with minimum-wage workers is even more stark. On average, one of Canada's one hundred highest-paid CEOs had earned a year's worth of minimum-wage work (full-time and full-year) by 2:23 p.m. on New Year's Day 2010.

But it is not just a rarefied handful of business leaders that are pocketing the dividends from growth. While it is true that the higher up the income ladder you go, the bigger the windfall, the top 10 per cent of Canadians have never had it so good. The past decade of fantastic growth delivered a concentration of incomes, wealth, and power that brings to mind a return of the Gilded Age of the late nineteenth century, complete with robber barons and the wishful mentality that anyone can strike it rich.

Canadians, particularly young families and recent immigrants, are pedalling as fast as they can – but are not getting ahead in the same way that their predecessors did. This generation of workers is better educated and working longer hours than did their counterparts a generation ago. Yet 40 per cent of the Canadian households raising children have lower earnings than similar families did a generation ago. Furthermore, the bottom 70 per cent of families raising children are taking home a smaller share of total earnings than their counterparts were a generation ago.[6]

Statistics Canada data show that, at last count (2008), just over three million Canadians were living below the poverty line, at the bottom of the income spectrum.[7] Another two million people were in the "near poor" category – with incomes up to 25 per cent above Statistic Canada's low-income cut-off (LICO) rate. This means that almost one in six Canadians was already struggling to get by in 2008, before the recession rocked the economy, especially in Ontario's manufacturing heartland.

Many of these people now qualify as the working poor. While we don't measure things in quite the same way today, something else that Senator Croll told the Empire Club in 1972 echoes eerily today: "Forty per cent of the working poor, those who work full time for wages and could do better on welfare, resist welfare and make do. We hear very little about these people."

The irony of the invisibility of poverty in our midst is that it disproportionately befalls a very visible population. Grace-Edward Galabuzi and Michael Ornstein tell us that we entered this recession knowing that the rates of poverty are stunningly higher among non-white Canadians, and newcomers – the very people that we will rely on in the coming years as the labour market copes with a record wave of retirements.[8] (See chapter 15.)

Most low-income Canadians do not stay permanently in poverty.

There is a churning effect as some manage to rise while others fall. However, it is getting harder to leave poverty behind even for those who work full-year, full-time. Ontario lost over 225,000 full-time jobs between the fall of 2008 and the fall of 2009.[9] The province's unemployment rate rose by more than 50 per cent, from 6 per cent to 10 per cent, in that period. It has since come down a bit, hovering around 9 per cent for most of 2010.

What is more, hours, pay, and benefits have been cut for countless Ontarians who were lucky enough to hang onto their jobs. Indeed, those who lost their jobs and found employment again would have been lucky if their new employment provided the same wages, benefits, and working conditions as what they lost. By 2009, food bank usage in Ontario had soared to over 350,000 people a month. Some 30 per cent of food bank users had at least one person employed in the household in 2009.[10]

Dave Bidini reminds us that far too many of us are teetering on the brink of poverty. Back in Senator Croll's day, a different cultural sensibility would have made more people conscious of how close we all are to that precipice. The phrase "There but for the grace of God . . ." was a common heritage among those who survived both the Great Depression and the Second World War.

Today many people are so absorbed in the struggle to stay afloat and get ahead that they have failed to observe how the focus of concern has steadily inched up the income ladder, from the homeless to the working poor and now, alarmingly, to significant parts of the middle class.

□

Since the 1970s, when Senator Croll's secretary used an electric typewriter and a pile of carbon paper to prepare his Empire Club speech, we have witnessed major changes in technology. Container shipping, air cargo, and satellite communications have contributed to a globalization of the job market. Aided by free-trade agreements, manufacturing jobs have migrated to faraway places. Sophisticated software has eliminated and deskilled service-sector jobs. Both globalization and technological change have helped to spur economic growth, at home and abroad. They have also put downward pressure on Canadian wages.

Add to these trends the predictable ups and downs of the business cycle, and it is small wonder that insecurity has been on the rise, steadily gripping more families in its clutch.

The massive recession of 1981–82 was barely behind us when the next crisis was unleashed, following on the heels of free trade with the United States. In the wake of the 1990–91 recession, an unparalleled social experiment was launched. It cut back income supports for all but seniors and relied more on market-based solutions.

While Canada did become a job juggernaut between 1997 and 2007, outpacing the rate of job creation among all G8 nations, that was not a result of the shift in public policy. While manufacturing exports initially led the expansion, the decade of robust growth was propelled more by Canada's growing role in the global supply chain as supplier of natural resources than by a growth in value-added production. The jurisdictions of Alberta, Newfoundland and Labrador, and Saskatchewan drove the boom, rather than the industrial heartland of Ontario. Indeed, during that decade of growth, 1997 to 2007, Ontario had the dubious distinction of being the only province in the country to increase the share of jobs paying less than $10 an hour – with that share climbing from 15.9 per cent to 17.4 per cent of all employment in the job market.[11]

Ontario, and the rest of Canada, were not recession-ready.

By late 2008, as the economic storm descended on Canada, less than half of the country's unemployed were receiving jobless benefits – and only one in three in Ontario.[12] Household savings rates were at levels last seen in 1938. Household indebtedness was breaking historic records, with the average Canadian household owing $1.40 in debt on every dollar of income, even *before* the crisis hit. That debt has since risen. It stands now at $1.49 owed for every dollar coming in the door, on average nationwide. The middle class is in trouble.

□

Since the recession began, the most rapid growth in employment opportunities came through temporary work (term or contract positions, seasonal or casual employment), and the expansion of self-employment.[13] It is not clear if these jobs are a stable platform for recovery in the labour market. Indeed, Statistics Canada's Labour Force Survey revealed that 139,000 full-time jobs disappeared from the job market between June and July 2010, wiping out in a single month a significant chunk of the 400,000 jobs created in twelve months of "recovery."

Nonetheless, by 2010 the federal government was singing a familiar tune: it is time to get out of the way of the economy and focus on the "real" job, tackling the deficit. Time for business as usual.

But the business environment is a little more ferocious than usual.

The wave of corporate consolidations that is sweeping markets all around the world is far from over. Sectors as diverse as mining, banking, media, manufacturing, and retail are seeing a shakeout of global proportions, with fewer players than ever calling the shots. In Canada the Davids are being squeezed out of a landscape in which only Goliaths can survive, a cutthroat landscape marked by high stakes and low prices. Businesses that have always been thought of as recession-proof, such as supermarket chains, are offering their unionized workers a 25 per cent pay and benefit cut for the privilege of continuing to have a job.

While many people think that the best social policy is a job, the sad truth is that, even in our affluent country, working full-time and full-year does not necessarily lift you out of poverty. Now even the middle class, for whom all politicians express such solidarity, is looking over its shoulder.

That is because good wages, pensions, and health-care benefits are increasingly being framed by business as unaffordable luxuries that hurt the bottom line; and few governments disagree. Suddenly the middle class worth nurturing is not the one that we already have in our own country, but the ones developing abroad, in emerging economies. Meanwhile, questioning multimillion-dollar bonuses for corporate executives is viewed as bad form, or an ill-considered critique of the free-market system.

Although an economic recovery is underway, the recuperation, for reasons both in this country and around the world, does not yet appear to have a trajectory that will lead to economic stability or security. Meanwhile history shows that poverty rises in the wake of recessions.

Canada entered this recession with the rate of child poverty just below the level it was at in 1989, when parliamentarians unanimously declared it a national disgrace in a nation as rich as ours (and vowed to eliminate it by the year 2000).

Statistics on annual incomes appear two years after the fact, and much has happened in this country since 2008. But if past recessions are any guide, between 750,000 and 1.8 million more Canadians will be counted as poor before that recovery is complete.[14] More than one in seven Canadians may have tumbled into poverty before this stage is over. Many of them will still be working.

The greatest increase in poverty will be among working-age adults (eighteen to sixty-four years of age), and the members of this large group will pull along the hundreds of thousands of children who live with them. For the first time in decades, we may also see a sobering increase in the number of seniors coping with low incomes, a phenomenon that did not occur in previous recessions but has already reared its head in the new numbers being released.

Some critics will argue that this recession was brutal but short, and that Canada has been recovering faster than most other nations, so that galloping poverty is not likely to be on the horizon. But two decades of stripping back income supports and putting more emphasis on market-based solutions repurposed the role of the state and left ordinary Canadians, suddenly faced with the most brutal recession since the Second World War, more exposed to the economic risks associated with joblessness than at any time since those earlier years.

The rise of the rich, a squeezed middle class, and the revival of the working poor: *this* is what we accomplished during the best decade of economic growth in forty years. In the coming months we will continue adding the nouveau poor to the déjà poor.

That kind of dynamic fosters a permanent, U.S.-style underclass and can destabilize communities.

□

Not surprisingly, some political leaders see the writing on the wall. They have started to turn their minds to the importance of income distribution and poverty reduction.

In 2002 Quebec became the first jurisdiction to announce a deliberate and multifaceted poverty reduction strategy in Canada. Between 1997 and 2007, before the impact of the recession, Quebec's approach and programming cut rates of child poverty by more than half, from over 22 per cent to under 10 per cent.[15]

Newfoundland and Labrador were next up, with Premier Danny Williams declaring in 2006 that his objective was to make that province a showcase for prosperity, and to deliver the lowest poverty rates in Canada. Seniors' poverty rates were 2 per cent before the recession; a strong economy had cut child poverty rates from 18 per cent to 6.5 per cent between 1997 and 2007; and poverty among working-age adults declined from 13.5 per cent to 7.5 per cent.

Since then four more jurisdictions have declared similar objectives: Ontario, Nova Scotia, New Brunswick, and Manitoba. They all took on the challenge *after* the recession hit. They are all aware that tackling poverty will cost money. They also know it will *save* money. Nevertheless, the road ahead is not clear, as governments at all levels grapple with falling revenues and rising needs.

In the past Canada summoned the political will to virtually eliminate poverty among our elders. At the same time we succeeded in creating massive amounts of wealth.

Over time the frictions between poverty and plenty have grown more gritty and unavoidable, raising moral and ethical questions that are particularly resonant for faith communities that have long been leaders in providing shelter and sustenance to the poor.

These good works continue to be *necessary*, but have never been *sufficient*.

Persistent Poverty gives voice to some of the increasing numbers of middle-class people being forced into destitution by joblessness and an inadequate system of public provision. In the pages that follow, people describe what it feels like to sit in their cars weeping as they try to summon up the nerve to approach the door to the church basement that houses the food bank.

The numbers of "losers" in the great competitive game are growing inexorably. A revolution of falling expectations represents a cultural shift from the time when Senator Croll pointed to the problems facing both aged and poor Canadians.

Back then a sense of possibility and public endeavour promised a better future. Today we have, until recently, seemed tragically paralyzed in the face of problems that are simple to solve. All we need is the political will. But will the economic crisis cut off the recent budding of just such a new political direction?

Ontario faces a large financial deficit wrought by a global meltdown with roots in laissez-faire, let-the-market-decide attitudes. What will our political leadership set its sights on now? The business cycle? Or the longer-term challenges that we are struggling to face?

By 2010 Ontario's social assistance caseload had jumped by 23 per cent in the wake of a major economic downturn. The Liberal government insisted on lowering the general corporate tax rate by 2 per cent and sticking to its pledge to cut corporate taxes yet again. It also insisted that it had to save money by cutting the Special Diet Allowance (SDA) that had enabled people on social assistance to at least make a serious attempt to pay for a medically prescribed diet associated with a health condition. (See chapter 9.)

Government is about making choices. In 1937 a Liberal Party labour minister in Ontario resigned amidst a Depression that was generating massive poverty. He could not in good conscience continue to serve in a cabinet that was sending Mounted Police to attack striking auto workers. In an eloquent letter of resignation, he made it clear why he had made his choice. He wrote famously, "I would rather walk with the workers than ride with General Motors."

His name was David Croll.

3 Working Harder Is Hardly Working

Anyone who has struggled with poverty knows how extremely expensive it is to be poor.
— James Baldwin

CARL, A DIVORCED MAN IN HIS LATE FIFTIES, had long enjoyed the comfort of his white-collar office job in an auto-parts manufacturing branch in Alliston, Ontario. After the automotive industry took a sharp downturn in 2008, Carl learned that he was the latest victim of a string of layoffs. He lived off his savings while searching for a new job, but to no avail. As his finances dwindled, he decided to move to Grimsby to be closer to his two grown children.

When he talked to us it had been two years since he had lost his job, and he was still unable to find work. At one point he was forced to sell his car because he could not pay for gas and maintenance. His community had no public transportation, and Carl no longer had any means of getting around other than walking.

"I always had a good job, lived in nice places," he said. "I am frugal, but after paying rent, clothes, haircuts . . ." His voice trailed off before he added, "I never dreamed of using a food bank."

Getting a job would make a world of difference for Carl, but his age had become a significant barrier. In his experience employers were not willing to hire someone in their late fifties or someone who has been out of work for two years, regardless of past work experience. He also lacked the financial support that would allow him to pay for transportation to get to job interviews.

"I need an economy where jobs actually exist for my qualifications. I need a social culture that values the skills of a man with my experience and will hire someone my age."

Inadequate wages. Unemployment. Underemployment. A lack of accessible education and training programs. These themes popped up again and again in the ISARC hearings across the province. Front-line service workers and other participants reported an increase in the "working poor" – people who work full-time, year-round, at low-paying jobs and struggle to get by. Securing employment is more complex than typing up a resumé and sending it around to prospective employers. To hold a job you need transportation, and child care if you are a parent, and money to pay for both. You need certification and skills to qualify for the position, and appropriate clothes to wear to the workplace. If a company, such as a restaurant, wants to maintain a youthful atmosphere, chances are it will avoid hiring older applicants, regardless of their experience.

A young mother who spoke to us in North Bay captured the struggle of the working poor: "My husband is working hard, and I enjoy being a stay-at-home mom. His job pays so little, minimum wage. Everything is going up. Hard work is not paying off. Up and down every month."

Melissa, another parent from North Bay, described her struggle with low-paying work: "Minimum-wage jobs are a problem in the system as you make too much to get a subsidy (for child care), but not enough to live half-decent."

"All your life you pay into the system and when you need it most, they give you a really hard time," said Graham, an Ontario Works recipient. The people in charge, he said, ask "Do you *really* need it?" As he told us: "It's hard to find a job when you're fifty-seven and there are lots of young people who are applying for the same thing. There are also people who are willing to work for less than minimum wage, and that undercuts others who really need that wage."

Those able to overcome these obstacles and find work often face the chaotic nature of low-paying shift work. They often have to deal with erratically scheduled shifts, and might find themselves being called in or forced to do overtime at the last minute. Precarious work creates increased instability and stress amongst those who are struggling to get by. For instance, Carrie, a single mother in Halton, told us how she held two part-time jobs, working seven days a week, just to make ends meet. During the week she worked in a high-school cafeteria. The stressful work atmosphere left her feeling exhausted when she went home to care for her daughter, Heather. She was trying to find a better job, but many of the available jobs in Oakville required late hours. Heather was at school during the day, and Carrie could not afford child care in the evenings. While Heather was at her dad's house on the weekends, Carrie was working at her second job. Carrie's ex-husband was on Ontario Works and had not paid child support in eight months.

"It feels like I am consistently having to do paperwork," Carrie told us. "Sometimes I think I would be worse off on OW, but sometimes it is so mentally draining dealing with my boss at work."

Carrie said she would like to have a stable work schedule, be employed at one job with reasonable wages. The stress of constantly working and searching for better employment had worn her down. Still, Carrie maintained an optimistic attitude and tried to focus on the positive aspects of her life. She was getting a great deal of support from her church. Even so, she said, "I don't like relying on my church all the time because I know there are a lot of people that also need help."

Carrie and many others are experiencing the labour circumstances known as precarious employment, which is "work for remuneration characterized by uncertainty, low income, and limited social benefits and statutory entitlements."[1] This kind of work can have multiple dimensions. It might be self-employment or paid employment; it might be temporary, permanent, full-time, or part-time. Precarious employment is also shaped by social context (a person's occupation and industry), social location (a person's gender, social, and political category), and the broader context of labour-market insecurity.

Despite significant economic growth over the past few decades, wealth has not been distributed equally; indeed, socio-economic classes have become increasingly stratified. Between 1980 and 2000 the richest – the top 1 per cent of all Canadian earners – saw a 113 per cent income increase from $156,757 to $333,382. Meanwhile, a quarter of Ontario's workers live on incomes below the poverty line.[2] A harsh reality is emerging in Canada's labour market: 37 per cent of all employment is "outside the standard full-time, permanent employment contract with a single employer." More and more workers are finding jobs that are part-time or contracted, or that come to them through temporary employment agencies. A significant gap in legislation leaves workers in precarious employment circumstances largely unprotected. In *Working on the Edge*, the Workers' Action Centre argues that current labour laws, regulations, and benefits are "based almost exclusively on a standard employment relationship developed after World War II, which linked decent wages, benefits, working conditions and job security to the full-time permanent job with one employer."[3] The international labour market, including Canada's labour market, has changed drastically over the past forty years. Employers strive to cut costs by channelling workers into part-time, contractual positions. People in precarious employment often have little social or political power, let alone legal ability, to challenge such conditions.

The unpredictability of precarious work had taken its toll on

Helena, a fifty-two-year-old woman in Halton, and her husband. Helena suffered neurological damage from two serious car accidents. She used to receive help from the Ontario Disability Support Program because her chronic pain was preventing her from working. After her common-law husband, Ken, found full-time work, Helena learned that she was no longer qualified for ODSP. Ken worked as a boat repairer, which meant that he was employed seasonally. When he was working full-time, he could make $1,000 in two weeks, but during slow periods work was hard to come by and money was tight.

Helena and Ken found themselves caught between ODSP and employment insurance, two systems that were incompatible with the timing of Ken's work. Helena said she could not go back on ODSP because she would have to prove that she and Ken had gone for longer than a month with low pay. They could have applied for EI, but the process would take six to eight weeks – and by that point Ken might well have been called back to work for a week or two, and he would have brought in too much money to qualify for assistance.

"I wish I could have kept my ODSP so that when my husband was not working I could help out," Helena told us. "I would feel like I was contributing financially to help support my family."

For Helena and Ken the stress of being strung up in a type of bureaucratic limbo had taken a serious toll on their relationship and mental and emotional well-being. Several years ago, when mortgage rates were low and Ken had steady employment, the couple had purchased a home. In 2010 Ken had been off work a lot. Helena was constantly worried that they would not be able to make their mortgage payments.

"Life at home is rough. We are constantly stressed."

Helena's spirits had suffered from being unable to contribute to the family's income. Her sense of self-worth plummeted. Her relationship with Ken deteriorated. The couple often found themselves caught in tense arguments about money. Once, in a heated shouting match, Ken lashed out and told Helena to go out and find a job.

"We've had huge fights over money," Helena said. "So bad that someone called the police and I had to go stay with my daughter. It was over money. It was so embarrassing, but you don't know how stressful it is."

Indeed, stress permeates all aspects of precarious employment. Struggling to get by on minimum wage. Absence of job security. Inability to qualify for benefits due to part-time hours. Juggling multiple jobs. Managing transportation and child care in accordance with erratic shift schedules. Precarious work undermines health by creating stress and instability and cutting people off from adequate health benefits and sick leave. Temporary agency workers may lose their jobs or fail to receive new assignments if they take multiple sick days. Precarious employment also damages health by limiting people's ability to take vacation or get personal support from others. Working long hours, evenings and nights, at multiple jobs – especially when schedules may be determined or changed with short notice – makes it difficult to relax or plan to spend time with friends or family.

Being unemployed, underemployed, or precariously employed cuts into your sense of personal worth and self-esteem. People living in poverty want to provide for their families, to support their children's growth and development, to be independent and self-sufficient. The struggle to overcome barriers to finding work increases stress and despair.

Larry, a man in his fifties living in North Bay, has felt trapped and been frustrated by his inability to find work. "There are no jobs available. I'm a landscaper and a drywaller. Nobody is hiring. My wife has to work three jobs. I don't feel like a man in my own house."

Noreen, another participant from North Bay, commented: "If you pay into CPP or EI, they deduct any payments. You are penalized for working. We need better incentives. I feel like I am an unproductive member of society. That doesn't make me feel good."

□

Gladys, a single mother in Halton, packed lunches each morning for herself and her three children as all of them headed off for the day. Of her children, two were in grade school and the other, the youngest, was in half-day kindergarten. While her children attended school, Gladys went to ESL classes. She had escaped an abusive relationship almost two years earlier and wound up in a women's shelter. She applied for Ontario Works and was able to get subsidized housing in a timely manner. She was unable to work full-time because her youngest was in school for only a half-day and she could not afford to pay for child care.

Gladys found a part-time job that would bring in an extra $700 per month. She was surprised to learn that Ontario Works would deduct 50 per cent of her earned wages from her next month's social assistance cheque. How could she afford to pay for child care during her shifts, as well as transportation to and from work, if she was not able to keep any of her earnings? After calculating that she would lose money each month, Gladys was forced to quit her job. She sometimes even considered going back to her abusive spouse. At the very least, he would offer a measure of financial security and could care for her children while she worked.

The issue of wage clawbacks was raised throughout the social audits (see also, for example, chapter 5). Clawbacks act as a disincentive to work and are a clear barrier to escaping poverty. That the government continues to punish its poorest citizens in this manner is unconscionable. The policy communicates an attitude of intolerance and mercilessness towards those who are impoverished.

Deborah, a former professional now receiving aid from the Ontario Disability Support Program – social assistance for those with disabilities – is trapped in a cycle of poverty due to the wage clawbacks: "It is discouraging to work when you are on disability. I can find some part-time work, twenty hours, but they take away 50 per cent of my earnings. Maybe if I was allowed to keep what I earn I'd be able to get ahead."

Dave, an ODSP recipient, commented, "ODSP gives you a stipend of $100 for working, but they take 50 per cent of what you earn. If we were able to keep what we earn, our standard of living would go up."

Dale, a Cornwall man who began to receive ODSP after being injured in an accident, was very supportive of the idea of his wife, Felicia, going back to university. Together they navigated a myriad of forms and applications to qualify for a loan from the Ontario Student Assistance Program (OSAP). Dale contacted ODSP to try to find out if they were allowed to borrow from the fund. He said he was told simply to bring in a form to find out how much of a loan Felicia could receive from OSAP. After eight months, all of the required paperwork was complete and it seemed that Felicia would be able to begin her studies in the fall.

The couple was shocked to discover that OSAP loans are deducted from ODSP cheques. Nobody had told them about the deduction. "We were under the assumption that we were allowed to borrow the money. Then we found out that they were deducting $700 off my [ODSP] cheques."

Dale sought an appeal and asked for a tribunal resolution with ODSP, but was denied three times. It took months to resolve these issues. Dale and Felicia were forced to reject the OSAP loan, and Felicia dropped her plans for university. In the experience of this couple it was confusing and counterintuitive that the government would punish people who were trying to get ahead in life and escape poverty.

"OSAP had no problem lending us the money. It's ODSP that is causing the problems. It's a constant struggle to get education."

For many of those who participated in the audits, a lack of formal education is a significant barrier to securing gainful employment. Alan, a middle-aged man from Niagara Region, grew up on a farm and struggled with school due to an undiagnosed learning disability. He never did learn to read. His teachers were unable to help him, and at the time the schools he attended did not have programs tailored to the needs of students with learning disabilities. Alan dropped out of school and worked on fixing up cars and tending to the farm.

When he spoke to us Alan was receiving Ontario Works and had been without steady employment for nearly a decade. He had a great deal of hands-on work experience in welding, electricity, and mechanics. But employers want to hire individuals who have their Grade 12 diplomas. Alan saw himself as being too old to go back to school, where it would be a constant struggle to understand anything in writing.

"I feel because of the diploma issue, people are victims in life because they are not given a chance. . . . Because of financial problems I face just to survive, I don't feel part of the community. Employers will not look at me now because of my education needs. More is needed to help put good people back to work. I just want to work."

Leo, a participant in Ottawa, faced some of the same challenges in finding employment. He lacked formal training and despite his past work experience had struggled to find a job. "I want to work, but I'm sixty. What should I do? Go back to university and graduate when I'm sixty-four? I know I'm safe, but I'm in a big mess. I need to have a job so I can pay for my health benefits for myself and my son."

Even if you are able to complete a training course, you have no guarantee that you will be able to find a local job in that field. Chelsey said she wanted to find a job in her field – administration and accounts – but few positions were available in York Region. She was considering switching careers and retraining for the health-care field, in hopes of higher job security. She wanted to be employed, independent, and able to provide for her two teenage children. Krista, a young woman from North Bay, went back to school to become a hairdresser. She received a 98 per cent mark for her work in the class, but had still not been able to find a job.

Daryl would welcome the opportunity to complete a retraining program, but was not able to cover the cost of the course he needed to take. Daryl and his wife, Natasha, who live in the Niagara area, were not on welfare. They were determined to provide for their three young children on their own. Daryl was also concerned about spending money on a retraining program and being unable to find employment in that field.

"Right now, committing a crime and going to jail offers better prospects for job retraining than staying out. In jail, the system pays for my training and feeds and houses me while I'm in training."

Teresa, fifty-two years old, moved to Peel District from Iroquois Falls when she was six. She worked in the printing industry for thirty-three years. The branch of the plant she was working in closed down, and she found herself unemployed for the first time in decades.

"I cannot find work anywhere. I have done retraining, job searching, and used agencies to find a part-time or full-time job, but no one will hire me."

Cheryl, a woman who spoke at the Waterloo hearing, commented that her life "just feels like a climb to the top of a hill that never has a top. There's no stability in my world."

Cheryl's comment, like many other stories shared at the hearings, evokes a chilling image of a Victorian treadmill. A long, large cylinder fitted with steps turns slowly in the middle of an enclosed yard. The authorities line the prisoners up and force them to walk endlessly upward. Ontario's workers – those who are precariously employed, unemployed, and underemployed – are struggling, taking step after step on a relentless economic treadmill. They learned the value of hard work long ago – indeed, more so than have many of those who are more fortunate – yet they remain prisoners of poverty within a system that does little to protect them.

4

Precarious Work: How Lax Employment Standards Perpetuate Poverty

Mary Gellatly

> There are great numbers of people who are in work but who, from a financial point of view, might equally well be unemployed, because they are not drawing anything that can be described as a living wage.
>
> – George Orwell, *The Road to Wigan Pier*, 1937

WHEN KALIL IMMIGRATED TO CANADA in 1981 he began years of work in computer services, doing repairs and technical support. Later on, as changes in an industry still seen as "high tech" reduced both its pay and demand for services, it became harder for him to get stable work at fair wages. He found himself having to adapt to changes in the labour market.

Kalil was hired by a company to service office equipment. He worked on a piece rate – $25 to service and repair equipment at the customer's site, $15 if the customer brought the equipment to the shop. When he had to go to a client's place it often took him three hours of travel to go there and back, plus an hour or more to do the work required, and yet he still only received $25. Many days he would make less than minimum wage. Then his employer started deducting money from his pay on the grounds that a customer had complained. The employer refused to prove that there really had been a complaint. Kalil told his employer that this practice was not right.

It was hard to make ends meet. "At home, I was buying two bags of milk every week because that is how much my kids needed. I started buying one bag a week. Half a cup a day for each one. Like orange juice, these are necessities."

At the same time, his boss asked him to train a new technician. "They only hire newcomers to the country," Kalil said. "I am the only one who was not a newcomer. They get low pay, the newcomers. They don't ask about health and safety matters and employment standards." He told us that the company hired a woman and asked Kalil to train her, and after he did they said, "We don't have much work for you. You are laid off." Even though his employers had regularly deducted tax, CPP, and employment insurance, the company refused to give Kalil a record of employment and termination pay. They argued that he was an independent contractor.

Kalil paid for night classes to become a truck driver. He quickly found a new job driving for a small company, which also saw him as an independent contractor and paid him a flat rate of $600 a week. Kalil got no benefits or overtime, vacation time, and public holiday pay, even though he considered himself an employee. His work time quickly crept up to fifty to fifty-five hours a week. Kalil was not paid for working more hours. Out of what amounted to $11 or $12 an hour, he had to pay his own taxes and CPP, leaving little left over to cover his costs as a parent with four children. Feeling there was little he could do, he moved on to another job.

The problems he experienced at work had an impact on his family life. His kids would call and say, "Daddy, we are waiting for dinner, when are you coming?" His son would ask him, "Dad, how is it going?" He found it difficult to answer. "How much can I talk to him? I don't want him to feel guilty that I am getting humiliated and troubled just to bring food on the table. . . . To make a living I have to cut the time from somewhere."

Kalil concluded that the changes in work were contributing to the disintegration of the family.[1] His experiences are typical of the challenges facing workers today. He faced violations of basic employment standards. He was receiving less than minimum wage, and working many hours without pay. He was misclassified as an independent contractor. If he spoke up for his rights, he could be fired.

□

Hard work is leaving all too many workers and their families struggling with job insecurity and poverty. More people are working part-time or on contract, often juggling two or three jobs. Workers face great difficulty in planning their daily lives and supporting families. Work hours and schedules are increasingly undependable. Many jobs today fail to provide supplemental health benefits, sick pay, or pensions. In 2008 Statistics Canada found that recent immigrants were more likely than were

Canadian-born workers to be forced into temporary or part-time jobs, to end up in jobs for which they were overqualified, and to be paid lower wages.[2] Employers shift work beyond the reach of government regulation to avoid minimum standards, and as a result workers, families, and our local communities and economy suffer. When labour standards are driven down or dismantled altogether, all of us – not just those at the very bottom – are hurt.[3]

Only 28 per cent of Ontario workers are unionized.[4] Workers who, like Kalil, are not unionized are not able to enforce their rights and negotiate wages and working conditions. When violations of minimum standards occur, workers must, as Kalil did for many months, absorb the lost earnings until they can find a new job. Often they are simply fired. Labour-market adjustment has effectively become privatized, and people like Kalil who least can afford it have to pay for training. With barriers to employment insurance and social assistance,[5] people are continually pushed into the next low-wage job.

Federal government policies press some people to stay in exploitative work until they can find another job – which all too often turns out to be low-wage and precarious. Work permits under the Temporary Foreign Worker Program tie workers to a single employer or require two years of employment before permanent residency can be sought. These immigration rules make it difficult for workers to fight against long hours at low pay in difficult working conditions. Workers seeking family reunification through immigration sponsorship must maintain their income levels to qualify for sponsorship. They cannot risk losing a job, even one that pays a poverty wage. For immigrants, fewer safety nets are available to help them enforce their rights. For example, social assistance is not an option when workers seeking to reunite families lose their jobs. That is because they cannot be on social assistance while sponsoring family members. While Ontario already has the lowest rates of employment insurance benefits for unemployed workers, recent immigrants and people in temporary work face even greater difficulties in attempting to get EI.

Gone are the days when workers had some degree of confidence that they could at least replace their current wages and working conditions if they were to risk enforcing their rights. Rising unemployment and downward pressure on wages and working conditions make it harder for workers to find replacement jobs when their rights are violated, making it all the more difficult for them to leave substandard work.

Increasingly unequal distribution of the rewards of work is leaving more workers like Kalil struggling to get by. Low wages have become a feature of our labour market. People working in Toronto full-time at minimum wage ($10.25 an hour) have earnings that leave them below Statistics Canada's low-income cut-off line.[6] Anyone working at minimum wage and supporting a family would earn well below the LICO. Recent immigrants are hit hard by low wages. Racialized women workers earn 47 per cent less than non-racialized male workers do, and 15 per cent less than non-racialized women workers.[7]

The majority of Ontario's over six million workers in more than 370,000 workplaces[8] rely on employment standards. It is workers in low-wage and precarious work who are least able to negotiate fair wages and working conditions with their employers, even though non-unionized workplaces are most in need of effective and inclusive employment standards. However, over the last three decades changes in the organization of work and the deregulation of the labour market have eroded employment standards protections.[9]

Employment standards set minimum terms and conditions of work, such as wages, hours, vacations, leaves, and termination and severance of employment. These standards reflect society's norms about what standards should be met in our jobs and labour market. Such norms include the ability to earn wages that are sufficient to live on and decent conditions of work that allow a person to balance work and family life.[10] Employment standards are supposed to establish a minimum floor of standards for those who have the least ability to negotiate fair wages and working conditions.

Not only is the *Employment Standards Act* (ESA) a central feature of labour-market regulation, but it is also an important social policy tool in fighting poverty. The Ontario government has stated that poverty reduction is a key goal of the Employment Standards Program. Poverty reduction will be aided through efforts to improve "the protection of vulnerable workers and to ensure fair workplaces by getting tough on employers who contravene employment standards legislation and regulations."[11]

Unpaid wages, overtime, and other violations are not just a matter of a few "bad apples" in the employment mix. The few studies that have been done confirm substantial formal ESA violations. In the late 1990s a federal government labour standards evaluation surveyed employers and found that 25 per cent of employers were in widespread violation of the *Canada Labour Code*, and 50 per cent were in partial violation. These findings were confirmed a decade later by Statistics Canada and the Workers' Action Centre.[12]

For years resources and staffing of employment standards regulation have not kept pace with increases in workers covered, and the complexity of working relationships. While the number of workers covered by the ESA increased by 24 per cent between 1997 and 2007, the funding for the Employment Standards Program decreased by 33 per cent. Even recent increases to the program in the 2009/10 budget leave the program over 10 per cent below the 1997 funding levels.[13]

With less than 1 per cent of workplaces being inspected for ESA violations, employers who flout the law face little risk of being detected. The only real risk of being found in violation of the ESA comes when an employee (usually a former employee) files a complaint at the Ministry of Labour.

Left unchecked, violations of particular rights become widespread over time. For example, violations of overtime and of the standards for hours of work cut a wide swath across many industries and sectors. With over one in ten Canadian employees working unpaid overtime (11.4 per cent), one management-side law firm estimated that this figure represents more than $22.5 billion in unpaid overtime and overtime premium pay.[14] Such widespread violations mean that workers have lost billions of dollars in unpaid wages and overtime pay. This income loss also means lost tax revenues and decreased economic stimulus through consumer spending. Poor labour-market regulation creates increased vulnerability for workers who are already vulnerable.

The majority of the government resources for enforcing employment standards rights still go to investigating individual complaints of employer violations. Researchers Ron Saunders and Patrice Dutil noted in 2005 that the "practice of dealing with compliance one case at a time is expensive and risks overloading the available capacity."[15] By 2010 the backlog in workers' complaints against employers for unpaid wages had grown to ten thousand items. Some workers have to wait more than a year to have the Ministry of Labour begin investigation of their complaints of unpaid wages and entitlements.

In May 2010, rather than providing better support for workers who would like to file employment standards claims for unpaid wages, the Ministry of Labour introduced Bill 68, *Open for Business*.[16] This curiously titled law would, if passed, create huge barriers for workers and put a greater burden on workers to enforce minimum standards. The *Open for Business* bill would require workers to try to enforce their employment standards directly with their employer *before* they can ask the Ministry of Labour to investigate employer violations; and new powers would allow investigators to mediate violations, thereby enabling settlements below minimum standards.

It is one thing to have labour-market standards and quite another to enforce those employment standards. As Chris Bentley, former Ontario minister of labour, said in 2004, "Rights without remedies will not be rights for long. Remedies that are not used are not remedies at all. . . . A more effective approach to ESA enforcement is long overdue."[17]

In response to calls from the Workers' Action Centre and its allies to improve the protection of workers, the Ministry of Labour committed in 2004 to conduct more surprise inspections of two thousand workplaces per year – an increase from virtually nil in prior years. Prosecutions of employers found in violation were also stepped up – yet still only about 4 per cent of employers who have been caught in violations face this legal action.[18] While advocates successfully pressed the government to increase funding to enforcement by $3 million in 2006 and to make a commitment of $10 million in the 2008 Poverty Reduction Plan, the reality is that the majority of resources for enforcing employment standards rights still go to investigating individual complaints of employer violations. In the relative absence of active enforcement of standards in Ontario's workplaces, the onus is placed on individual workers to enforce their own statutory rights.

□

Explicitly or tacitly, over the past three decades employers have adopted strategies for work organization that evade core labour laws and create a legal distance between the employer and workers. This is an evasion aided and abetted by the remarkable growth in precarious work and the limitations of the labour laws, regulations, and benefits established after World War II (see chapter 3).[19] The historic exclusion of certain types of work organization from regulatory protection (for example, independent contractors) has created incentives for employers to move workers into new forms of work. Employers may call it "externalizing" the costs and risks of front-line jobs. But this time-worn practice of contracting out areas of their businesses that could be done in-house is hardly new. This was a common practice in the garment and manufacturing sectors long ago, at the beginning of the twentieth century. Found in most industries today, employer strategies include:

- using temporary help agencies to indirectly hire workers for short- and long-term employment;
- outsourcing work that is considered low-skilled and labour intensive to intermediaries operating as contractors (which is what large companies do with cleaning, janitorial services, and food services);

- nominal subcontracting, using intermediaries to "payroll" existing staff who overnight become employees of subcontractors (which is what major newspapers have done with newspaper carriers, or communications companies have done with technicians or salespeople);
- misclassifying workers as independent contractors to treat them as exempt from labour laws;
- shifting costs of doing business onto workers (as in Kalil's case, where wages were deducted when customers complained, or with cleaners who are required to pay a fee to get work and have to pay for their own cleaning supplies and equipment).

Employers may argue that these strategies are necessary because of global economic integration. While it may be that some local manufacturers struggle to drive down their costs in order to compete against firms located elsewhere, globalization does not satisfactorily explain the new employer practices in Ontario. Many employers and industries engaged in outsourcing, indirect hiring, and misclassifying workers are in sectors that have distinctly local markets – restaurants, janitorial services, business services, construction, trucking, home health care, warehousing, and the packaging and manufacturing of locally consumed goods.

New employer practices aimed at evading and eroding employment standards also create regulatory headaches. Misclassifying workers as independent contractors, outsourcing work to temporary help agencies or other third parties, using bankruptcy to shed liability for employment standards: all of these tactics create challenges for both regulating and enforcing standards.

The outdated labour laws trap people in poverty, denying fair standards to all workers. That is why the Workers' Action Centre and groups from across the province have been organizing to press the Ontario government to update the ESA to protect all people who work in temporary, contract, and unstable work. This organizing has resulted in some steps forward. In 2009 the Ontario government adopted changes to the ESA to protect people working through temporary help agencies. Now all temp agency workers are entitled to public holiday pay and protection against being charged fees for work, among other improvements. In March 2010, live-in caregivers won protections against recruitment fees and unscrupulous recruiters. Still, much is left to be done.

Workers remain resolved to continue pressing the provincial government to adopt a minimum-wage policy in which no one managing to work full-time and full-year will still be living in poverty. Then too,

Ontario's most vulnerable workers need a minimum-wage policy – including a minimum wage indexed to inflation – that will bring them over the poverty line. Our outdated labour laws must be modernized to ensure that all workers are protected by basic minimum standards that reflect the social goals of decent wages and working conditions. The lives of workers and their families must be sustained. Moreover, we need our government to do its job and ensure the enforcement, at the very least, of minimum standards.

5 Ontario Works: How Did This Happen to Me?

> These were stories of people who held good jobs, executive posi-
> tions, who had owned homes. Due to numerous factors out of
> their control – the recession, job layoffs, illness, family breakdown
> – they ended up in poverty. They never imagined that it would or
> even could happen to them. — ISARC rapporteur

IN OUR 2010 SOCIAL AUDIT, again and again our rapporteurs listened to stories of unexpected misfortune that had forced people to turn to social assistance, to struggle to survive on such a low income, and to surmount daunting barriers while trying to escape poverty. Once poverty knocks you down, the stories go, it is difficult if not impossible to get up and off the floor.

"The various rules and regulations of the different support programs can actually worsen a person's chances of getting out of poverty," a York Region rapporteur told us. "For someone on social assistance, who may have had limited education, and who may be facing a variety of health concerns, this challenge can be overwhelming."

This rapporteur, a former teacher and private-school administrator, heard the exasperation of front-line workers who found themselves unable to provide the necessary help because of the maze of rules. He noticed a common thread: rather than offering them the means of becoming self-sufficient, the rules trap people in a cycle of poverty. What's more, the system never seemed to provide enough support to enable receivers to get by.

"In many cases the financial support provided was clearly inadequate to meet the needs of the individual in terms of appropriate housing, clothing, and food – surely very basic needs. This financial pressure was clearly constant and made it very difficult for people to try to do something more positive with their lives."

This volunteer had experience in these matters. Long-time Liberal

activist Charles Beer served as Ontario's Minister of Community and
Social Services in the late 1980s. As soon as his party regained office in
2003, the new government brought him in as chief of staff to the Minister of Health, who was faced with running Ontario's biggest-spending
and most politically sensitive department.

Aside from the lack of resources and overabundance of red tape that
concerned Beer and so many others whom we met when we took the
pulse of the province's communities, one striking theme emerged. People who had never imagined that they would be in an insurmountable
state of financial distress are increasingly finding themselves waiting in
the welfare office. In 2008, and thereafter, this bad dream became a
reality as more and more people lost their jobs, finding themselves with
reduced incomes and forced to cut personal and household expenses
while living on employment insurance. When their EI ran out, they
would find themselves having to apply for social assistance. When they
found how little assistance they would receive each month, they were
overwhelmed. "How did this happen to me?"

Pete was born in Canada, but in 2006 he and his wife, Vivian, relo-
cated to the United States, where he had found a great job. During his
time in the States, Pete was making $100,000 a year. He and Vivian
enjoyed the finer things of life. Ironically, during that time they made
donations to agencies fighting poverty. Everything changed when Vivian
developed terminal cancer. Paying for the treatment in the United States
cost Pete and Vivian their house and savings. After Vivian died, Pete,
now in his early sixties, returned to Canada, where he offered assistance
to his bipolar son by helping to care for three grandchildren. At the
York Region community hearing, Pete shared his reflections on his life's
dramatic changes.

"If you would have told me three years ago that I would be here
today, I would not have believed you.... Truthfully, I didn't really
understand poverty at that time because, like most people, I was
uncomfortable [seeing] people living in poverty."

When he first returned to Canada and began caring for his family,
Pete refused to go to the food bank out of pride. He was determined
to make ends meet on his own. He quickly realized how difficult it is
to stretch a meagre social assistance income to provide for his family.
In 2009 Pete went to a food bank in the York Region for the first
time.

"That day I sat outside in my car and cried. My pride made it difficult to go in. I knew that I needed to go in for my grandchildren. People
who find themselves in a situation like I am ... it doesn't take long

before they lose themselves, their dignity, self-worth. . . . Anyone can end up in a situation like me."

☐

Ontario Works (OW) is Ontario's name for social assistance, or welfare. It got the name as part of a rebranding exercise carried out when the Harris government slashed welfare rates in 1995. OW provides a monthly stipend broken into two portions: a monthly shelter allowance ($364 for a single adult) and a basic living allowance ($221 for a single adult). That comes to $7,020 a year. The rate increases for people with children. A sole-support parent with a child under eighteen gets $572 for housing and $341 for basic living: $10,956 a year. That parent also receives Ontario and federal child benefits, so a woman in this category would have $16,775.04 to support herself and her child each year.

When Ontario's Liberal government introduced the Ontario Child Benefit in 2007, it took away annual "Back to School" and "Winter Clothing" allowances for children. In 2007 the Ontario Child Benefit was only $500 per child per year. Barbara, a single mother on OW, talked about her struggle to budget on this level of income – about how the changes to the OW system interfered with her attempts to control expenses. As she put it, "Ontario Works is just bare bones."

Since October 2003, when the Liberal government was first elected, Ontario's cost of living has risen by 13.46 per cent, but Ontario Works stipends for adults have risen by only 11 per cent. While the government cites a 20 per cent increase in social assistance, this is true only for parents who have children living at home, with the increase occurring primarily through federal and provincial child benefits. In 2010 a single adult on OW had 40.86 per cent less purchasing power than she or he would have had in 1995.[1]

According to Statistics Canada, people living in a rural area are considered to be "poor" if their income is less than $14,000. People living in urban areas need even higher incomes. The $7,020 received annually by that single adult on Ontario Works is simply not enough to maintain a healthy diet and provide a modest, but safe, accommodation. James, a man on OW in Niagara Region, is frustrated with the never-ending struggle to make ends meet on $585 a month. "This is criminal. I don't understand why this is okay in such a wealthy country as Canada. I think we should stop punishing the poor. People on assistance should have a living wage."

Miriam, a mother of three children in Markham, has chronic liver disease. She receives a monthly social assistance payment of $1,500, but $1,100 of that amount goes towards rent (she does not live in subsidized housing). This leaves $400 for everything for herself and her three teenage children – for food, basic hygiene and cleaning products, transportation, phone, clothing, and medications not covered by the Ontario Drug Benefit Program. Miriam struggles to pay for high-school registration fees, extra fees for art and science classes, and extracurricular activities. Without help from her extended family, she would not be able to make ends meet.

"There is no money for gifts," she told us. "At Christmas time, the choice is always between paying the bills or gifts for the children."

Many ow recipients reported the stress caused by this kind of harsh choice. Pay the rent? Buy food? Make sure your son is not excluded from a school trip?

Cynthia, a woman in her late fifties in York Region, described her predicament. "At one time we had almost paid for our house. Then we lost our jobs and had to sell the house. I am diabetic . . . what do I do? Do I pay for my meds, rent, or food? I can't pay for everything, so I have to choose."

Patricia, a single mother in Newmarket, captured many people's plight: "I have a $200 deficit every month already." She worried about changes in the rules and regulations that could further reduce her income.

The prospect of scraping by on such a paltry income is even more daunting because before applying to Ontario Works applicants must liquidate virtually all of their assets. Many of these people have just experienced a tragic event: separation and family breakup; job loss; being kicked out of the family home; physical or mental illness. Or they might need to care for a dependent family member. It could be someone turning eighteen after living for years as a Crown ward. Reeling from an upheaval, these people learn that to qualify for help they must use up all of their savings except for the equivalent of a single month's social assistance. A single person can only have $585 in assets. A sole-support parent with one child can have $913.

Sybil watched as a storm tore through her Simcoe County home. She was unable to get insurance money, and was ineligible for legal aid that could have helped her to negotiate with the insurance company. She experienced an emotional breakdown. Social workers attempted to assist her as she recovered, but she was new to Simcoe County and not all that familiar with the area. She was discharged to the local Elizabeth Fry Society home, an emergency residence for women.

Now, because she had no permanent address, Sybil was not eligible to apply for Ontario Works. She could not even pay for bus tokens. She was confused. How could she get an address without first having an income to pay for rent? How could she find a job without transportation and money? Sybil tried to see if she could take the Elizabeth Fry bus to get to a job interview, but it was not available on the morning of her appointment.

The process of using up personal assets and applying for ow strips a person's sense of self-worth and dignity. People who spoke to the social audit described how uncomfortable they were with a scrutiny of their assets and expenses that is almost forensic in nature. When Alfonso met with ISARC in Ottawa, he described a time when his caseworker came to his house, asking questions about his belongings. He resented the invasion of his privacy. He felt as though the authorities were treating him like a child. Other participants echoed Alfonso's sentiments. They described their own experiences in having to respond to demands that they justify any extra expenses. They talked about the humiliation they felt about conditions – like being forced to notify caseworkers if they were leaving the province.

"It takes whatever dignity that you have and it dissolves it," said Norm, from Ottawa.

"The ow application process was the most degrading thing I have ever experienced," reported Michael in Barrie. "Even talking with the caseworker over the phone creates fear and panic. They speak to me in such an accusatory attitude, with allegations of fraudulent behaviour."

The meagre stipend, coupled with the requirements about using up virtually all personal assets before getting assistance, puts low-income people in a bind when they have to deal with large expenses. It becomes impossible to cover utility bills, medical costs, or emergency transportation (including ambulance costs, which are covered by the Ontario Disability Support Program but not ow), or, as usually required, to put down the first and last month's rent. The social audit heard repeatedly from people forced to turn to lenders like Money Mart or the Cash Store to cover urgent costs, even though these outfits charge dizzyingly high interest rates.

Anton, a young man from Ottawa, described the effect on self-esteem of his struggles to live from paycheque to paycheque, unable to save. "I'm a proud person and to admit that I'm on the verge of bankruptcy is hard. This isn't where I imagined I would be when I was twenty."

☐

One of the most counterintuitive policies of Ontario Works is the "clawback." The government deducts from social assistance the various benefits, child-care payments, student loans, and wages that people receive. This policy serves to lock low-income people into a perpetual state of poverty. Rapporteurs and participants from all of the community hearings consistently urged an end to this practice. As the ISARC rapporteur in York Region put it, "Not harmonizing the operations and processes of these different assistance programs continues to be an impediment to sound social policy."

The term "clawback" originated (at least in this policy area) in 1998, when Ontario clawed back the National Child Benefit (NCB) from parents on OW and disability benefits. Later, when the federal government increased this benefit through the Child Tax Benefit (CTB), it did not allow provincial governments to deduct these funds from monthly welfare cheques. The hope of provincial and federal governments was to provide a regular income for parents, so that they would have sufficient income to provide for their children whether the parents were working at low-wage jobs or on social assistance. Parents who are working without any social assistance benefits receive full federal and Ontario child benefits.

Despite previous increases to monthly income through child benefits, many parents told us that they had seen no significant change in their monthly incomes during 2009. While the increase to the Ontario Child Benefit was announced in the provincial budget as $42 per child per month, some parents on social assistance saw as little as $2 per month per child. OW was being restructured as an adult-only benefit. Child benefits were received by parents with low incomes whether the adult was employed or on social assistance. Parents thought they were promised a higher monthly income, but did not realize that OW was changing and that other portions of their cheques would be reduced.

Another clawback occurs when a court orders a non-custodial parent to pay child support. For a single mother, even when – as often happens – the child support money fails to arrive or is paid late, her social assistance cheque is still reduced unless she can prove that she received no child support. The irregular payments mean another round of phone calls, documentation, and visits to caseworkers. For a parent who has no phone, limited money for transportation, and no contact with the non-custodial parent, the experience is an administrative nightmare.

The voice of one single mother, Vera, rose as she described the anxiety of trying to get a letter from her former spouse who had not paid child support. "I don't even know where he is! What am I supposed to do? Live on even less money?"

Student loan money from the Ontario Student Assistance Program (OSAP) is also deducted from monthly social assistance cheques. Paige, a mother who receives OW, was very discouraged about how hard OW's restrictions and regulations made it to make ends meet. Her daughter, Christina, was accepted into college and applied for OSAP. Christina would use the OSAP money to pay for books and tuition. But even though the money would be used for education, not food or rent, OW staff told Paige that if her daughter accepted the OSAP loan, an equivalent amount would disappear from the family's monthly benefit cheque. Discouraged, Paige said, "I come out poorer than when I went in."

Several parents described the OW policies dealing with young adult children. They learned that their older teenage children would have to leave home because OW expected the kids to earn money and contribute to the family income. Martha, a mother of a recent high-school graduate, resented how OW dictated the way in which her family should live.

"My eighteen-year-old daughter is not ready to be on her own. What do I do? How can I help her, especially if she's not in my home? How do we survive?"

OW recipients who do find employment face wage clawbacks. The program deducts half of all earned incomes from their cheques. Not only does this policy act as a disincentive to find work, but people who do find a job can end up with a decreased monthly income. Finding and keeping a job also costs money. You have to have appropriate clothing, and pay for transportation to the interview and then to work and back. Janelle managed to find a job in Toronto but soon had to quit. She could not afford to pay for work-appropriate clothing and transportation when all her wages were being deducted from her benefits.

Sandy, in Durham Region, struggled for years before being able to get off social assistance. "It's a fight. It took two years to get off assistance. They make it harder for you to get off assistance and discourage you."

When she met with ISARC, Sandra in York Region was receiving $585 from OW, plus help from the Special Diet Allowance due to her wheat and dairy allergies. Food banks could not provide the specialty foods that she needed. She was working part-time and earning about $900 a month – which meant that $450 was deducted from her next OW cheque. She paid $500 per month in rent for a shared apartment. Because she only had just enough money for rent, food, and transportation, she was concerned about the loss of her Special Diet Allowance money after the government announced in the 2010 provincial budget that the program would be discontinued. Sandra was very fearful of any changes that would reduce her fragile income.

"How can I get ahead when half of my employment income is deducted every month?"

The clawbacks have made many people so fearful that they do not file income tax returns, even though they might be eligible for HST rebates, child benefits, and money from overpaying taxes. None of these items are clawed back by Ontario Works, but some recipients are not aware of this and assume otherwise. Some single adults in particular are not aware of HST rebates. If they do come to realize in June or July that the only way of receiving the federal or provincial child benefits is to file an income tax form they will find out that the free community tax clinics have closed for the season. If they are unable to fill out the form themselves, they are forced to pay a tax firm to do the job.

A service provider in Toronto commented, "The flexibility in income support is gone. There are too many clawbacks in different ways. There are just too many stupid rules."

☐

Caseworkers are the key to making social assistance work, yet they are overloaded and stressed. In one region caseworkers described the difficulty of working in office cubicles with limited privacy. Veteran workers remember a time when home visits were more relaxed and OW applicants could get some privacy. There was more time to do the interview, especially if the recipient had emotional issues. Waterloo caseworkers have one hour in the morning for phone calls from the recipients on their caseload. Then they schedule appointments ranging from a half-hour to an hour for the rest of the day. There is an annual consolidated verification process, in which another caseworker goes over the same information with the OW recipient to make sure there are no irregularities. Recipients need to bring their bank statements, credit card statements, and accommodation expenses. Some people quickly sense that they are not trusted and feel stigmatized.

Rapporteurs in Chatham-Kent reported that most caseworkers were sincerely trying to help those in need. Still, others seemed to need some type of sensitivity training to help them understand the plight of the people they encounter on the job. A caseworker's personality and attitude can have a dramatic impact on people who are on social assistance. Both rapporteurs and recipients noted an apparent staff shortage resulting in overwork. It becomes difficult to build helpful relationships. Without decent rapport, distrust and fear can easily develop.

In Durham Region one recipient, Brian, concluded that there are those who get help and those who do not. While some recipients get lots of time, others get very limited service. Brian was frustrated by having to meet with different caseworkers each time he went to the office.

Many low-income people cannot afford telephones – which presents a problem for caseworkers who, for instance, might need to quickly remind a recipient about a required interview. Many low-income people have pre-paid cellphones or phone plans with time limits. It costs money when they are put on hold for any length of time, so it is difficult and expensive to connect with a caseworker who is taking another call or busy with another client. While ow offices have telephones that can be used to call caseworkers who are in the same building, the recipient must still get to the office to make the call.

☐

Ontario Works recipients who fail to adhere to specific regulations risk being labelled "non-compliant." Compliance could mean bringing in a medical form, a receipt, or a bank statement. It could also mean making an appointment with a professional or providing a prospective employer's signature. Since the steep economic downturn of 2008, social assistance offices have seen significant increases in applications. Waterloo Region caseloads increased by 38 per cent, and the local government had to hire new contract staff. An experienced caseworker noted that the training process, coupled with the new caseworkers' desires to follow the rules, tended to generate "black and white" decisions, with the newly hired workers hesitant to give beneficiaries a bit of extra time to comply.

Documentation is a key issue for ow recipients. Many of them fear that they will be stripped of their benefits if they stand up for their rights. The system itself issues automatic letters and intimidates by threatening legal processes. When a letter arrives, it protects the system but its complex language alarms the beneficiary. These communications generate fear and anger. Caseworkers receive anxious calls from recipients asking, "Will I get my cheque?" Recipients fear the appeal process. There is a single recurring message: "Comply." ow recipients become discouraged as they encounter the staff and system. They become depressed and give up.

Jacqueline in Halton Region was disgusted by the process. "I hate being labelled non-compliant." Celine in Chatham vents, "Some case-workers think that when you are in poverty you are automatically stupid."

Susan, a woman in her forties living in Cornwall, said she constantly had to provide written documentation to her caseworker. If she did not produce the documents, her cheque was withheld. Other recipients reported that case files were lost, misplaced, or simply not available to a caseworker. Beneficiaries had to replace documentation, often at a personal cost. Susan was exhausted by the system. "Ontario Works doesn't work. My whole life is a fight. You are guilty until proven innocent."

People applying for and living on Ontario Works are distressed when they have to repeat their stories again and again, particularly because caseworkers often change. Heather, in Simcoe County, said she felt like a second-class citizen. "I realize they are overloaded with clients. They could take time to listen. . . . Each time I call I get a different caseworker and it is very frustrating. I feel like a beggar."

□

Although OW was ostensibly designed to get "people back to work," a 2006 task force (Modernizing Income Security for Working Aged Adults, or MISWAA) reported that it was not in fact doing so. The MIS-WAA taskforce included business people, social policy analysts, social justice advocates, and community workers. Its report highlighted significant issues that by 2010 had still not been addressed.

- Asset limits that are too low for OW recipients.
- The need for flexibility in assisting low-income Ontarians who need benefits; the need for additional income for themselves and their children.
- The major gap between parents with children and single adults, with single adults being much poorer on OW – which distorts work incentives for single adults.
- The need for medical, dental, and drug benefits to continue until beneficiaries have received benefits through employment – the loss of benefits can lead a recipient to choose not to seek a job.
- The 50 per cent clawback in employment income, which serves as a strong disincentive to work.[2]

In 2007 a Toronto-Dominion Bank and Royal Bank report declared bluntly that OW is a "mishmash of tax and income support policies which penalize Canadians on social assistance who take a job."[3]

Ontario Works is an utter failure that produces cynicism, fear, and feelings of worthlessness. In Halton Region ISARC heard various statements to this effect. "We are useless to society." "I feel labelled and I hate it." "We are guilty until proven innocent."

This system works against people who are looking for work. People cannot receive funds to assist with clothing, grooming, buying work boots, and meeting other employment-related expenses until they can verify the existence of an interview or a job. What happens if the interview is the next day? There is often no time or transportation to pick up the cheque and purchase supplies. To attend an interview parents need to arrange for child care – and find the money to pay for it.

Ontario Works creates dependency. Medical benefits need to continue until a beneficiary qualifies for employers' benefits. Recipients need to build some cash reserves during the first months of employment. Clawing back 50 per cent of the wages makes it impossible to build up financial resources and purchase essentials. Throughout the social audits, recipients of OW said they wanted to work. The system needs to actively support them without punishing them when they do find work.

Paulina owned a home in Oakville and had a good education and a good job. When she lost her job, she went on employment insurance. Then EI ran out. She went for three months with no income. She applied for OW.

When, as she said, she "walked in clean and fresh and presented in a business mode," the response was, "You don't need help."

Paulina felt that no employer was going to take a chance on her. The competition was tough. She was finally accepted on OW. Caseworkers requested information that Paulina did not have available to her at the time. When she met with them to try to explain her situation, she was called a liar. Her file was suspended. Her house was sold without her signature. Ontario Works wants her to sign money over to them once she receives money from the sale of the house. She was left with no money and no place to move.

"I have reached out to everyone for help, but people think I'm kidding because I still smile."

6

The Disorienting Disability Support Maze

We are made to feel like powerless children.
                    – Rachel, ODSP recipient, North Bay

S USAN, A YOUNG WOMAN FROM RICHMOND HILL, had the misfortune of being bitten by a tiny tick carrying the bacteria that transmit Lyme disease. The tick bite happened before the disease was recognized in Canada as a disability. She was unable to work, but her doctor failed to tell her that she was eligible for social assistance. She later learned about the Ontario Disability Support Program (ODSP), but by that time she had already gone on Ontario Works, which meant that she had first needed to use up all her savings, RRSP, and cash (see chapter 5). "If ODSP had been made available to me earlier," she told us, "my health would not be in this condition and my finances definitely would be much better." In the end ODSP finally accepted her application.

Just to become eligible for the Ontario Disability Support Program is a long and difficult process. About 50 per cent of the applicants are self-referrals. Others are Ontario Works recipients. While OW client services workers can encourage recipients to apply for ODSP, they cannot make a referral or take the time to assist with the application. People without support or with mental health and/or addiction issues have a difficult time pulling together an application, which requires details about personal disabilities plus a physician's form. Unfortunately many Ontarians no longer have a family physician. Several other certified medical professionals can fill out the medical form, but the medical professional doing so needs to have known the applicant for several years.

At the time of ISARC's 2003 social audit, getting onto ODSP took somewhere between twelve and fifteen months. The rejected applicants went straight into an appeal stage with an adjudicator, and Legal Aid Ontario won between 75 and 90 per cent of the appeals on behalf of these people. This application and approval process has been improved in the last few years. Now, once the application forms are completed, there is a wait of three to five months. If the applicant is rejected, a request can be made for an internal review by senior ODSP staff in Toronto. Many "second looks" approve the applicant. If still rejected, the applicant can appeal to an adjudicator.

Many people find it difficult to navigate the process of filling out an application and submitting it. The work involves filling out several forms, and a doctor or an approved medical professional has to complete one of them. Applicants often need to pay to have the forms filled out. If an applicant is at all disoriented due to emotional or mental health issues, the process becomes that much more difficult.

Tim, in Toronto, received advice on how to obtain ODSP. He described the process: "Everyone told me I had to get a psychiatrist to get on ODSP. Well, finally I got a lawyer who helped with the process. Everyone needs an advocate."

A Durham social worker, Bob, explained the transition from OW to ODSP: "They have programs at the welfare office, but you must have an advocate if you have a mental health issue and want to get service." If a person has a disability, ODSP ($1,042 a month for a single adult) provides more income than OW ($585) does, and it also assists with additional services and funds for returning to employment and provides support for medical and related costs. The 50 per cent deduction for every dollar earned does not begin with ODSP until the recipient has earned $500. ODSP vision, dental, and medical benefits continue until the employer's benefits are equal to or better than those gained through ODSP and the Ontario Drug Plan.

In Cornwall, Sue remembered the ODSP application process. "I had to fight for five years to get a pension. They kept turning me down. There's a big lack of information from the government." In Wallaceburg, Anna said, "Before I could qualify for ODSP, I was told I would have to use the $10,000 I had from selling my house. I now worry if I'll have enough to live on in my older age."

As causes of their disabilities, ODSP recipients listed workplace injuries, mental health issues, physical illnesses, automobile accidents, botched medical procedures, and physical or sexual abuse. People with addictions were formerly denied disability benefits, but a successful human rights case resulted in addiction being added as a qualification for ODSP.

Disabilities take many forms, and circumstances lead to further challenges and injury. Harry's learning disability meant that he struggled with reading and writing. He had a drinking and drug problem and had trouble finding work. When he did find work he was often hired for dangerous jobs. After two incidences – falling from a roof and getting into a car accident – he became permanently disabled. Later on a bank foreclosure led to an eviction from his deceased parents' home in the country. Eventually finding himself homeless in Toronto, he finally became sober and found a basement apartment.

Frank ended up on the streets of Toronto after the ODSP office lost his application. He, too, became free from drugs and started advocating for himself. He was finally accepted. He moved to Acton to stay clean and safe. He left the care of a psychiatrist who wanted to put him on drugs, and then joined Narcotics Anonymous. He concluded, "If I get enough sleep, exercise, and shop efficiently, I can regulate my condition. I don't need drugs."

ODSP recipients are grateful for their monthly income, but expenses rise faster than income. In North Bay, Charles bluntly described the dynamic: "Expenses go up. Income doesn't keep up." His friend Greg tried to get ahead, but, Greg said, "For every dollar I make, I lose half. I never know what my income will be. Why punish people for working?"

Max was paying $800 for rent and had $200 a month for all his other needs. He said his needs were clear enough. "Give me $1,000 per month on top of my $1,000 ODSP benefits and I'll go to school. I need the support now, and then the government won't need to support me for the rest of my life."

Rodger, in Cornwall, was not able to work at a regular job and was trying to manage his budget carefully, finding ways of paying rent and having good food. "I can't afford cheese. Every year I have to cut, cut, cut." He was struggling each month to find $25 for crucial medications not covered by the Ontario Drug Plan.

Brook and his partner were trying to get by on ODSP in York Region. Their shared accommodation meant less shelter allowance for each of them, but their main problem was obtaining medications not covered by the Ontario Drug Plan. Brook had suffered a head injury; his partner had cancer. "We need over a thousand dollars a month to pay for all the meds that we need." They were relying on the local food bank.

ODSP recipients want social assistance staff to respect them as human beings. In Renfrew County Hannah said, "The social assistance system seems to be less 'client'-focused and more 'process'-focused. For example, people on disability have to have their forms signed by doctors. Yet how many low-income people have access to doctors? This adds to the despair many feel living in poverty."

Chad, twenty-eight years old, struggled with mental health issues while acting as primary caregiver for his mother, who had suffered from recurrent strokes. He was frustrated. "I am treated like a number and when I'm told to take a number, I get pissed off."

Max had the same problem, but found support through the Fred Victor Centre in Toronto, where ODSP recipients founded a friendship group to deal with their social isolation. Max is grateful for the chance to help and be helped. "I am labelled, certified with mental illness. I have to accept it. I do have lots of anger issues. I find acceptance in this group."

Isolation was a common concern among the disabled people who were trying to get by on social assistance. "I can't handle stress," said Tony, a single man living in Barrie. "I can't work and people don't always understand that. Some people just don't want to deal with people on social assistance. The problem with mental health problems is that relationships with friends dwindle and your family may abandon you."

A rapporteur in Simcoe County recognized that support workers could be a big help in breaking down the barriers of isolation. "Thankfulness for supportive agency workers, friends, family, and church was expressed by more than half the interviewees," said Kristine. "Like housing, the more stable and helpful their support network, the better able people are to cope and to be positive." Kristine reported that "some workers aren't helpful, others are angels."

Mary, in Niagara Region, had struggled after being physically and emotionally abused as a girl. Her only source of income was ODSP, but it failed to provide enough for her to cover rent, utilities, and groceries. She noticed that people were judgmental about her smoking habit. "When my food runs out, coffee and cigarettes keep me going. Then I feel people are judging me because I'm thin and they think I'm a crack addict. I'm not." Cigarettes cost less than food and are an appetite suppressant. As she said, with a tinge of bitterness, "I'd like you to walk a mile in my shoes before passing judgment."

Like isolation, communication is a daunting issue that confronts disabled people on social assistance. It is compounded by red tape. "You have to find out everything on your own," said Laurie. "They don't volunteer the fact that you can receive help with transportation. You have to learn to navigate the system and learn what is out there." Bob found out quite by accident that he could get help to obtain a York Region bus pass. "No one ever told me. It's made a big difference for me."

Communication can be a one-way street. Judy said her welfare worker was consistently demanding information from her, but she was not getting the information that she herself needed. "I felt like there was no respect." But contrary to her experience on Ontario Works, Judy found that ODSP client services workers were more caring and better able to help with the maze of issues she faced. They seemed to have more time and more ways of assisting recipients. But it is still a hit-and-miss system that is often just as intrusive as it is helpful. Joanne from North Bay explained, "My worker asks about my assets all the time. She will ask about my wedding ring, my children's bank account, and if I inherited money."

The week before the Halton Region social audit, a mother with two teenagers described her struggles with both communication and isolation. Jill had not filled out her ODSP forms correctly and received a letter expelling her from the program. She was referred to a psychiatrist. She had already asked her children's father to raise the kids because he had decent housing and a good income. "I don't want my kids to suffer. They need things other kids have." She found herself crying all the time because of her loneliness and financial insecurity. "Will I become homeless? I find myself looking for places where I could sleep if I lose my money or am evicted."

Sarina said she would become panic-stricken whenever ODSP client services workers called, frightened that her funding would decrease. She had managed to set herself up as self-employed in Cornwall. "They cut back on my funds so much one time that I didn't eat for a week. I fainted while working with a client."

In North Bay, Dorothy explained, "They [ODSP workers] should know how to treat people properly, but the computer system doesn't provide diagnoses for caseworkers. They don't know what they are dealing with."

Indeed, the ODSP system does not provide client services workers with diagnostic information for their clients. The information is kept confidential in Toronto. The recipient must inform workers of any disability. This policy is intended to prevent stereotyping while helping workers keep an open mind with respect to clients. But the process sets a difficult dance in motion. Disabled people provide information to the system but do not realize that their caseworkers know very little about them. This provokes distrust. Since many people on ODSP have serious mental health issues, client services workers can have trouble building a trusting relationship with clients. The result can be crises in their offices. One ODSP staff person noticed that the office's 911 calls had increased significantly in the last several years.

Distrust increases when ODSP recipients experience a sense of disrespect. Isabel, in Renfrew, felt judged as a lazy and incompetent money manager and was unfairly accused of defrauding the system. The process undermined her self-esteem and her sense of financial security. "How could I stay motivated to improve my skills or move to financial independence?"

We live in an advertising-sodden world in which people see themselves as customers. Low-income people with disabilities are no exception. David told the North Bay hearing that he just wanted the system to treat him fairly. "It's a calamity if I don't receive my cheque. Anyone is upset if payroll screws up your pay cheque. I'm a customer. I should be treated well." Paul, in Durham Region, would like to see "designated workers to deal with consumers who have mental health issues." He saw himself as a consumer "assisted by workers who effectively help us obtain what we need." He pointed out that the ODSP office was not accessible for the physically challenged.

"It sounds like the system is very paternalistic," said a facilitator at the North Bay social audit. "Does the system treat you like children?" John quickly replied, "I wouldn't do this to my kids – the way the government treats low-income people, no way!" Robert entered the discussion: "We are made to feel like powerless children." Rachel explained, "We don't go out often because we feel guilty. Sometimes workers find out and they question us."

Elsie, in Cornwall, blind and self-employed, was working from home. "Some workers are rude and verbally abusive," she told us. "I'm intelligent. Why do they think they can abuse me? Then they send me information I can't access. It needs to be in Braille."

Beatrice had been living in Quebec, helping her mother. She said that in Quebec she could make $200 a month without it affecting her cheque. She still wanted to find work. "But it's hard when you can't read. I did have tutors and I tried. They got frustrated with me and I quit."

"When I make too much money, my ODSP is taken away," Andrea explained. "It's really de-motivating when not working actually results in my receiving more money." The social audit heard repeatedly about what Andrea described as "oppressive red tape." She remarked, "It's part of the stigma. You feel like you're on the bottom of the list."

Judy, in Niagara Region, wondered, "What the hell am I fighting for? It's a day-to-day, even hour-to-hour struggle. I keep sane by volunteering in a local apiary. I don't want to lose my mind." She would like to see politicians experience "our way . . . see how you make out." She suggested that the best time for them to do this experiment would be "the last week of the month when the money is gone." Susan, in York Region, also said she would like others to face the "daily struggle with not enough money to survive. I'm tired of living on Kraft dinner. It is not unusual for me to go several days without food. How can I eat healthy when all the money goes for rent and utilities?"

The telephone is one of the necessities that some people eliminate. As June, a parent in Barrie, told us, "According to the government, a telephone is a luxury item. As a parent, I need a phone." The phone is also necessary to connect with the client services worker, especially when the recipient needs information or wants to appeal a legal notice that comes in the mail.

Transportation was a problem cited by many ODSP recipients in the community hearings. Karen lived in a rural part of Niagara Region, which has "an utter absence of public transit. The only way to get around is [by] foot, bicycle, or taxi. Taxis are prohibitively expensive for people on welfare. Simply getting to the doctor's appointment can be an ordeal." (For more on rural transportation issues, see chapter 16.)

Some people walk everywhere, reported several participants in Orillia. This was a common theme in both suburbs and the country. The poor do not have cars, said people in Durham, a collection of sprawling suburbs where shopping and services are geared for those with cars. Greg remembered walking from Ajax to the Whitby office only to find out that the counsellor had forgotten the appointment and was not there. Clara, in Wallaceburg, struggled to get around. "I don't have a car. I walk. Pushing a [grocery] cart to bring things home is getting more difficult, especially in winter."

"What do I do? I am disabled and need taxis, which are not covered by ODSP," said Charles, who was using a walker. Pete in Waterloo Region said he "got infected feet from walking so much. I needed the bus."

In Niagara, Susan needed a car to get her two children around but her car needed new brakes that she could not afford. "I know I'm driving an unsafe car, but there's no public transportation and I don't have any alternative."

Jane chose to keep her car on the road. "I'd be isolated without it. I missed a payment for car insurance and they cut me off. It now costs me an additional seven dollars per month to get [insurance] back on."

One rapporteur asked audit participants about their vacations. ODSP recipients laughed. "We aren't allowed to leave the region for more than two weeks without telling our client service worker. Where would we go? We can't even get around the city because our money goes for rent and food." Waterloo Region social services workers wondered about priorities. The local Grand River Transit offered special rates for university and college students. Why shouldn't there be a low rate or free pass for people with low incomes, especially now that many buses are accessible?

Cynthia, in Kent County, explained how long it was taking to get about. "Transportation is a full-time job. It takes me four trips to get the same amount of groceries a person can get with a car. It takes me an hour and a half to get to the hospital. Just getting around sucks the life out of me."

Jim, in Oakville, said he had a truck – but he had to borrow the five dollars for gas to come to the Halton social audit. He said it cost him forty dollars twice a week to drive to his physiotherapy appointment. But ODSP would only provide nineteen cents per kilometre for the use of his truck. Transportation can also be crucial in finding and keeping a job. Andrea, in York Region, remembered, "I found a job once with the YMCA. I was hired, but the problem was transportation. I had to take four buses just to get to the job."

Breaking the cycle of poverty requires accessible and affordable transportation for jobs. People on disability benefits are no different from anyone else. They need to get to medical appointments and grocery stores. They, too, have friends and family they need to visit. Rapporteurs across Ontario were astounded to realize how the lack of access to adequate transportation is so profoundly important for people with low incomes. For rural people, public transportation is often totally unavailable. In cities the high cost of riding buses erodes food and rent budgets.

James demonstrated the frustration of many who testified at the 2010 ISARC social audits: "We don't know how to live like this. Who put the hole in the safety net?"

Government seems to regard disabled people just as nineteenth-century Victorian authorities saw charity cases – the "deserving poor." Disabled people get a slightly better deal than the "undeserving" people on Ontario Works. Still, each of the province's thirty-six public health units is legally required every year to survey Ontario's communities to calculate the costs of a Nutritious Food Basket. As the Association of Local Public Health Units explained in a 2009 letter to the Premier: "When these costs are added to average rents for the same area, it becomes clear that people on social assistance throughout the province are being forced to choose between paying rent and buying food. They are sending their children to school without breakfast or lunch and are relying on food banks for survival."[1]

A year later, just as ISARC was conducting the social audit, the ODSP Action Coalition was organizing a similar effort. The organization heard stories from 236 ODSP recipients in sixty-one communities and in July 2010 produced the report *Telling Our Stories: Disability Should Not Equal Poverty*. It noted: "People on ODSP are often isolated by their poverty because of stigma and lack of resources to participate in community life. Rules inhibit spousal relationships, leaving many feeling destined to live alone. Lack of opportunities in terms of employment, education, transportation and basic community activities leaves many people on ODSP excluded from society and frustrated at not being able to contribute."[2] The resulting summary is a remarkable reflection of what ISARC heard. The stories represented but a fraction of the experiences of the 370,000 people with disabilities and their families who depend on social assistance for their primary source of income.

7 The Affordable Housing Deficit: Out of the Cold

A FFORDABLE, SAFE, AND SUPPORTIVE HOUSING is a crucial key to reducing and eradicating poverty. Ontario has far too little of it, and the market is simply not ready, willing, or able to provide it.

After listening to stories from urban and rural Ontario, a Simcoe County rapporteur wrote: "If a person's housing situation is good – meaning stable, safe, affordable, and nice – then the other aspects of life are better and stress is reduced. The opposite is also true. If housing is not good, then stress is increased and other pressures in life increase and create more problems and chaos."

As rents in the private market rise, more and more people struggle with inadequate, unsafe, and unaffordable housing. Others become homeless or are forced into temporary emergency shelters. These desperate situations came up repeatedly in the social audits.

We learned of growing waiting lists for affordable housing in Brantford, Chatham-Kent, Cornwall, Durham, Halton, Hamilton, Peel, Renfrew, Simcoe, Toronto, Kingston, Waterloo, and other regions. In York Region, 48 per cent of tenants and 27 per cent of homeowners spend more than 3 per cent of their incomes on rent or mortgage payments. People on Ontario Works and the Ontario Disability Support Program are often paying 90 per cent of their already meagre incomes for rent. Many individuals and families at the social audits reported having trouble paying for rent and nutritious food. Rents are increasing faster than income. As Margery in Kitchener asked, "Will more people be hungry or homeless?"

Shelter allowances through Ontario Works and the Ontario Disability Support Program languish below average rents. For a parent and two children, the ow shelter allowance of $620 is far below $978 per month, which was the average in Canada Mortgage and Housing Corporation's 2010 survey of rents for a two-bedroom apartment in Ontario. In Toronto the average cost of a two-bedroom apartment is $1,134 per month. Shelter allowances on ODSP are $791 for a parent with two children. The remaining $358 on OW and $207 on ODSP must come out of the basic living allowance, which pays for food, clothing, transportation, and other expenses.

Ruth was living with her husband and four children in a Burlington condo when her husband left her for another woman. Although she tried to keep the family home, Ruth was forced to move when the bank issued a power of sale. Her children wanted to remain in Burlington, so she found a townhouse even though it stretched her budget to the breaking point – she wanted a decent home for her children. She applied for a housing subsidy but faced a two-year waiting list. At least she was on "the list" as she struggled to make ends meet. She finally won child support from her husband. Unfortunately he had a low income and did not pay much. Still, she said, "Every little bit helps."

When she read that Habitat for Humanity was building homes in Burlington, Ruth applied to and then volunteered with the charity. She will always remember the two women who came to tell her that she and her family had been accepted for a new home. By the time she talked to us she had been living there for three years, but she was quick to remember others who had not received this opportunity. Now she had a commitment to increasing public awareness of poverty and the lack of affordable housing in her community. She asked, "When will others have the chance to break the cycle of poverty?"

Another mother, Barbara, rented a semi-detached home in Halton Region, but it was so cold on winter nights that she and her children went to bed with their clothes on. The basement had so much mould that she tried to get the house condemned. Now, for the past three years, she had also been living in a Habitat for Humanity home, thankful for her garden and bedrooms for each of her children. But she was worried because she did not have the money necessary to keep up with normal household repairs. "What if I had a serious plumbing or electrical problem? How do I pay?"

We found that there were urgent needs in Simcoe County. By 2010 the number of affordable rental housing units had recently increased from 2,400 to 3,200, but the waiting list had still climbed from 617 to 841. Many individuals and families were no longer placing themselves on "the list" because waiting lists could be eight to ten years long. In Waterloo Region, the waiting list was over 4,000 households – including over four hundred individuals with mental and emotional health issues who needed support services to live independently. They had to meet categories of urgent need, level of income, gender, age, adaptability of the unit to the disability, and level of support services needed. Many people in need were deciding not to apply because the waiting time was over four years. The waiting time changed quickly for some individuals in the case of hospitalization or an emergency. Their situation became a higher priority. Yet others waited even longer.

A Cornwall rapporteur expressed the consensus of her social audit group. "The waiting list was overwhelming. Those who rented paid more monthly than those who had a mortgage. Renters didn't have the necessary funds to put a down payment on a home." Describing tenants in the private rental market, the rapporteur said, "More money was going to housing than if they had owned a house!"

"If I can become homeless, there is not another person in the world who can't become homeless," said Harry, a middle-aged man in Brantford. "Even people who are wealthy are very close to being in poverty: one death, one broken relationship, one loss of a job. There are not a lot of choices for housing, and it often means living next to people who are smoking pot and crack."

York Region, where 90 per cent of the homeless were men, had only one shelter, with twenty-five beds for men. A man could only stay in the shelter for six weeks. After that the staff will help him find rental housing. Or start a shuttle to find an emergency shelter somewhere else.

Emergency shelters cost more per month per resident than keeping a person in an apartment. Rapporteurs asked, "Why do regional and municipal governments support living in shelters rather than apartments?"

In Waterloo Region, it costs $42.50 per night or $1,275 per month for an adult shelter bed. Canada Mortgage and Housing Corporation reports that a one-bedroom apartment in the region averages $712 per month. Hostel residents and staff are concerned that there are too few safe, affordable apartments and rooms for residents who are exiting shelters. In fact, 24 per cent of the emergency shelter residents in Waterloo Region in 2009 returned to the hostel within the same year. This "revolving door" syndrome means that personal issues remain unaddressed and adequate housing is nowhere to be found. The Support to End Persistent Homelessness (STEP Home) program has helped shelter residents settle into appropriate apartments, resulting in a 7 per cent decrease in former residents returning to the emergency shelters. Still, the region's Homelessness and Housing Umbrella Group 2010 report card gave Waterloo Region a C grade ("No Improvement") in the category of absolute homelessness.[1]

One man, Allen, talked about being chronically homeless in Toronto for the past fifteen years. "There was nothing for single people. The rooming houses were terrible, with lots of people with addictions and other problems. The houses themselves were not up to building code."

In the Greater Toronto Area (GTA) suburbs Sam's teenaged son could not use the same homeless shelter as his father because males under twenty-six years of age were not allowed in it. So the son lived in a tent while Sam stayed at the hostel for six weeks before his allotted time ran out. Sam reported on his conversation with OW staff: "I can't get welfare because they told me that my son and I can't live together and collect. We can't get it [OW] anyway because I don't have an address." Sam wanted to work, and his son wanted to finish high school. But how could they find housing, the first step towards Sam finding a job and his son returning to school?

Some homeless people resort to the life of a "couch surfer" if they have friends who let them sleep in their apartments. In Halton, Rosemary slept on her daughter's couch and kept her possessions in the trunk of her car. Some people just remain on the streets. But as Jim, living on ODSP in Toronto, reported, "I have a friend who has a son and they come to my place to shower while they live on the street. I used to live on the street, so I know what that is like." Others also reported street people who were "shower surfing" in their apartments. But how long can people rely on their friends for a couch or a shower?

In some shelters drug and alcohol abuse by residents can make the living situation feel decidedly unsafe. Rooming and boarding houses, especially those with low rents, can also be unsafe places.

Rachel, a young York Region woman, felt trapped. "When you are a single person on your own, there's not really a lot of help for you. If you are a woman without children, they will move you around to different shelters. Every six weeks I was moving." She later found a family who rented her a room in their house. Rachel finally felt safe and comfortable, only to learn that the family was moving. What would her next step be?

Pamela, a single woman on OW and working part-time in York Region, explained: "People don't want to rent to you if you live in a shelter. People don't want to rent to you if you are on disability. . . . Eventually I got a job and rental unit, but it was a struggle to get there."

Annabel in Toronto was humiliated. "I've been offered housing that's not even decently clean. And there's a lot of housing I can't get into because of my low income."

In Kitchener employed people use an Out of the Cold program during the winter because they simply cannot pay the private landlord's standard first and last month's rent. Many cannot afford private-sector leases. Moreover, many landlords do not accept social assistance tenants.

Some families have moved to rural areas because of the lower rents there. In Mountain there are no shelters for men. Subsidized housing – with the inevitable waiting list – is reserved for people over fifty-five. Once they have moved to the country, people face transportation issues and high utility costs for housing that is often poorly insulated. In Renfrew County, rents have recently increased from $500 to between $700 and $1,000 a month. Meanwhile, audit participants reported deteriorating housing conditions. Tenants are often "going without furniture, proper flooring, or basic services, such as electricity, because they could not afford to pay the bills." Rural housing became a bad dream in a beautiful setting.

In the fast-growing city of Barrie, the search for shelter after an emergency meant a radical change for Betty and Bill. "This was a hard transition because we were used to living as a family – man, wife, and children. Now we don't have that and have to live in a small room in a rooming house." Families without housing are usually separated in different shelters, one for men and another for women and children – or sometimes neither. A young teenager was caught in a bind because he could not go to the women's hostel with his mother or to the men's hostel with his father. The pressure to move out of the shelter was so intense that families would take anything available. With the long waiting lists for subsidized housing, where could this family find a home?

The Toronto West audit recommended transitional housing, which is now an option for single adults in only a few areas. Steve was given a stark choice when he was discharged from the hospital: he could go back to the streets or to a boarding house. He chose the boarding house, but wondered about the support services that would be available. He hoped that transitional housing would give him time and prepare him for the next steps. "You lose your choices when you are poor."

Jacob, a young man in Toronto, described his situation: "A bachelor apartment cost $600, maybe $700 a month in Parkdale. Rooming houses are terrible. People steal your food, mess up the bathroom, get drunk and bring friends home. My socks and underwear were stolen from the laundry. How do I pay a high rent on my ODSP of $1,092 per month? It would be worse if I were on $585 from OW. Am I supposed to steal?"

Richard reflected on his experience living on Ontario Works money in downtown Toronto. "The people most affected by slum landlords were on fixed incomes. If you were on welfare, $400 a month was going to pay the rent in a rooming or boarding house and you had less than $185 for everything else. So you ended up in these kinds of places. You tried to better yourself while you're in the hospital, or in custody [stop using drugs, get on the proper medications, go back to school, partici-pate in Alcoholics Anonymous and other activities], but when you got back out, you were back in the same old situation again." Many revert to old behaviours and once again found themselves in a crisis.

John, a middle-aged man living in the Peel area, was advised to head for Toronto to find housing. He wanted to live in Mississauga, where he had family, friends, and a job. "My paycheque was not what it used to be, and I didn't want to go on OW. I just wanted some support for hous-ing. I was worrying myself sick because I had no options."

In Waterloo Region, some apartments are overcrowded with too many people in too few bedrooms. One extended immigrant family try-ing to get ahead financially had to organize a sleeping schedule, with one person using the bed during the day while others worked; the oth-ers used the bed at night. This allowed twice as many tenants in the apartment.

Mark and Nancy, a married couple in their thirties in Niagara Region, were determined to avoid social assistance and live on Mark's income of $20,000. Nancy looked after their three children. With fully three-quarters of the family income being absorbed by rent, Nancy had little left over to cover the cost of hydro and other necessities. She learned to negotiate late payments, but lived in constant fear that the hydro would be disconnected.

Even for people with low rents, paying for utilities becomes a major problem. Some of the people we heard from found reasonably priced accommodation, but the houses were heated with oil and not covered by the Share the Warmth program that helps low-income people with some utility bills. Sara's rent in a rural house in Waterloo Region was an affordable $357, but filling the oil tank cost $279 per month for ten months. She simply did not have the money. With her part-time job and Ontario Works income support she was fine during the summer. "I turn off the furnace and hang the clothes outside to dry. Children love to play outdoors. I use less water." But she dreaded the coming of winter, when she would have to use all of her part-time paycheque to pay the oil bills. "How do I win?"

Gendered family dynamics can prove problematic. Judy reported that she needed to pay a $450 deposit for hydro in Orillia because there was no account in her name. She had paid the bills and managed the family finances, but the account was in her former husband's name, and she had no credit.

Delinquent landlords who neglect basic maintenance are also a source of anxiety for tenants. "You'd have to live in the place I'm living to believe it," said Michael, who lives in a York Region basement apartment. He had been trying to get the landlord to complete basic repairs. "The owner doesn't care. It's only an investment."

Some people did not see rent controls as a solution. Janice in Halton stated that rent control "fosters poorly maintained buildings and makes it unattractive for owners to add rental units. It unnecessarily lowers the rent to the entire population." She was concerned about getting landlords to fix up their apartments.

Adam, a single male with mental health issues, recalled his experiences. "I've been treated like a third class citizen, especially when it comes to the *Landlord and Tenant Act*. . . . I need connections to help deal with this stuff." Many tenants were not only afraid of evictions, but also wondered if they had rights. "Slum landlords should be made accountable for maintaining their properties," urged Peter from Chatham. Joyce cited examples of problems in her apartment building: "Steps are broken in my backyard, which is a danger to my children."

An eviction can be costly to both the ousted tenant and the landlord. A 2005 study by the Canada Mortgage and Housing Corporation found that an eviction in a major Canadian city costs the tenant an average of $2,234. These costs include moving expenses, establishing a new residence, losing belongings, and paying damage deposits. As a result of these costs, tenants who are afraid of eviction tend to avoid reporting unpleasant or dangerous conditions. "Tenants don't report things like leaky basements," said Phyllis. Landlords also bear a financial burden during an eviction due to legal fees, repairs, and unpaid rent. Social-housing landlords pay an average of $3,000 for an eviction, while private-sector landlords pay nearly $6,600. Other potential costs include emergency shelters and addiction or mental health treatment. It seems ideal for all parties to practise eviction prevention in order to keep tenants in stable housing. The CMHC research recommends "rent banks" (where an outstanding rent is paid directly to the landlord on behalf of the tenant) to support tenants and landlords in achieving this goal.[2] The Ontario government supported rent banks in both the 2009 and 2010 budgets.

Ahmed and his family arrived in Canada with hope and determination. They have enjoyed the opportunities available here, but have struggled immensely with finding affordable housing. The family has had to move several times, and each time the move costs money that they do not have. The family would like to locate permanently to York Region, where Ahmed works. For them, housing has "posed one of the most cruel problems" for the family. "Low or no income forced us to overcrowd ourselves into tiny basements."

People who attended the Toronto West audit commented that many areas, such as Regent Park, Flemingdon Park, and Jane-Finch, have concentrations of low-rent housing and are isolated. "People don't leave the neighbourhood, except for the high-school kids, who were shocked when leaving. Isolated communities don't work and will never work. We needed integrated housing and mixed neighbourhoods," explained one participant. One of the people who attended the Parkdale audit discussed gentrification – the process that sees the disappearance of affordable housing as higher-income families move into an area. With gentrification people leaving shelters and mental health programs have even less choice when it comes to finding housing. "There is nowhere to go for them."

Judith in Barrie described the stigma she experienced. "I live in a dump. I would like to move because areas with low-income housing are not the best place to raise my children. But I can't get the money for other housing." Explaining that housing is always an issue for women, she argued for mixed housing throughout the city. Betty has chosen to live in Burlington to avoid the stigma of low-income housing in Hamilton. She felt that many places she could afford in Hamilton were dirty and unsafe. What were her alternatives? She stayed in Burlington with her two daughters and tried her best to manage.

Throughout the audit process, ISARC heard from people who regarded affordable and safe housing as a crucial ingredient for people seeking to escape poverty and establish themselves. It will take sustained and committed support from all levels of government to eliminate the affordable housing deficit that Ontario has accumulated since 1995. It is a fantasy to think that private-sector developers will, on their own, build what so many with so little need so desperately. It is only through public provision that Ontario can provide the housing that is the key to any meaningful strategy for poverty eradication.

8 Housing Strategy on the Brink: The Time Has Come

Michael Shapcott

O VER THE COURSE OF SEVERAL BUSY MONTHS in 2009 more than 1,100 people crowded into meeting rooms from Thunder Bay and Ottawa to Windsor and Toronto. The meetings were so well-attended that eager participants often spilled out into the street. Organizers arranged for tents and sometimes had to set up additional meetings. Cookies and coffee were consumed, big ideas were tossed around, and practical solutions were raised. Over three hundred groups and individuals joined a vigorous on-line discussion, submitting detailed and pragmatic solutions to a problem that is at the heart of Ontario's persistent poverty.

The focus of all this fevered attention was the much-anticipated, and long-delayed, affordable housing consultation launched by the Ontario government in the late spring of 2009. A call to consult does not always generate such positive interest. Cynics and people who have often participated in the public consultation merry-go-round sometimes dismiss these exercises as "brain-sucking" because they engage people in discussion and channel their energy into meeting after meeting with no apparent result.

But for the millions of Ontarians who are precariously housed, plus community leaders, housing experts, and advocates, the provincial housing consultation was too important an opportunity to be wasted. The Housing Network of Ontario (HNO), an alliance of provincial and local housing leaders, was formed to ensure that the consultation was used to maximum advantage – to ensure that the effort as a whole contributed the best possible ideas to the process.[1]

Sadly, a year later – on the eve of the date of the promised release of Ontario's long-term affordable housing strategy – the Ontario government casually announced that its plan would be delayed until fall 2010.

Does it matter? What difference would a provincial housing plan make, anyway?

A made-in-Ontario housing plan has not existed for almost two decades. In this regard Ontario has fallen far behind other provinces. As of 2008 Ontario was spending fewer provincial dollars per capita on housing than was any other province. The waiting lists for affordable housing across the province have been growing longer (up 10 per cent from 2009 to 2010). The number of Ontario households in core housing need is increasing. In recent years the provincial government's housing initiatives have been inadequate and poorly targeted.[2] This problem was underlined just as the 2009 consultations were winding down. In November 2009 Ontario's Auditor-General reported on the province's affordable housing programs, noting several critical concerns.[3]

The provincial Auditor-General found little co-ordination among the three provincial ministries that oversee more than twenty housing and related programs. Ontario lacks "established and dedicated staff resources . . . monitoring the success of its funding programs in achieving their desired impact." This is linked to the Auditor's finding that several recent major housing initiatives, including the 2005 Housing Allowance Program and the ongoing federal-provincial Affordable Housing Program, are poorly designed and targeted, and do not benefit those who need the help the most. Ontario cannot properly account for $330 million in federal housing funds by demonstrating that this money has actually been spent on affordable housing initiatives. And, finally, the Auditor showed that the expiry of federal housing agreements (the accelerated withdrawal of federal housing subsidies that was put in place in 1996 but would only start to bite deeply in the years following 2010) will create a major financial hole for Ontario. It threatens thousands of low- and moderate-income households.

□

Poor housing is not simply uncomfortable and uncomfortably unaffordable. It is directly linked to poor health.[4] People living in insecure housing, together with those who are homeless, bear a heavy burden of increased illness and premature death. In addition to the personal cost, poor housing disrupts communities and puts a drag on local and regional economies. Poor housing is a big – though often unacknowledged – burden on governments because it increases the costs of health and social services.

Increasingly, community and municipal leaders, faith groups, business organizations, and academic specialists have recognized that a good home is not only a fundamental human need, but also a basic requirement for healthy, inclusive, and prosperous communities.[5]

The overall number of Ontarians who are precariously housed is staggering. Fully 1.3 *million* households pay 30 per cent or more of their income on housing. The 30 per cent mark is the official definition of unaffordability. Indeed, 118,675 of those households are officially overcrowded, and 79,290 of them struggle with substandard housing that requires major repairs.[6]

Several factors drive the high level of housing insecurity. The cost of energy rose by 50 per cent over the past decade. Rents have risen faster than inflation, while tenant household incomes have been stagnant or declining.[7] Even though a good supply of ownership housing and low interest rates have in recent years allowed some higher-income renters to move into the ownership market, ownership affordability has been eroding in the wake of the economic meltdown.[8]

As of 2009, the median renter household income was $27,892 – almost identical to the level of income required to cover the average market rent of $26,130 (the annual income required to pay no more than 30 per cent of income on housing). This means that about half of all renters do not have enough income to pay for their housing and still have enough money left for necessities such as food, medicine, transportation, clothing, education, child care, and other expenses.

As an increasing number of low- and moderate-income households were effectively priced out of the private rental and ownership markets, Ontarians looked to the provincial government to take leadership in ensuring access to affordable housing.

Yet provincial housing programs have been clear-cut over two decades – with Ontario generally following the lead of the federal government in the continuing erosion.[9] In 1993 the federal government stopped all funding for new affordable homes. In 1995 Ontario stopped all provincial funding for new affordable homes. In 1996 the federal government announced its plans to download most housing programs to the provinces and territories. In 1998 Ontario launched its own downloading of costs to municipalities.

As housing insecurity and mass homelessness began to rise during the 1990s, the federal government announced a series of short-term, patchwork measures, and the province mostly followed the federal lead.

In 2001 the federal government and all the provinces signed the Affordable Housing Framework Agreement. Initially set for five years, the federal government promised $1 billion to be matched by the provinces and territories. Ontario finally signed onto the deal in 2005 – and the provincial rollout has been slow since then.

In June 2005 the federal Parliament authorized $1.6 billion for new affordable housing, including off-reserve Aboriginal housing, with $1.4 billion allocated in the spring of 2006. But it would be almost two years later, in spring 2007, before Ontario signed on for its share of the affordable housing funding, and a year after that (fall 2008) before it took up the federal dollars allocated for off-reserve Aboriginal housing.

The federal "stimulus" budget of 2009 allocated $2 billion for new affordable housing initiatives over two years. Instead of the provincial delay that followed the 2001 and 2006 federal commitments, Ontario quickly announced that it would deliver its share of the federal funding. Ontario seemed content to let the federal government set the pace on housing, with the province's financial support steadily dwindling relative to other provinces and territories.

Ontario's Public Accounts show that provincial operating spending on affordable housing has been mostly stagnant in recent years[10] – and most of the operating dollars actually came from the federal government (see Figure 8.1). In 2009 unilateral provincial operating dollars were below the 2003 level.

Figure 8.1
Operational Spending on Affordable Housing

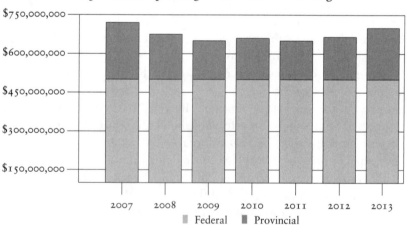

The provincial capital dollars for housing have risen since 2006, with both federal transfer dollars and unilateral provincial dollars growing, according to Ontario's Public Accounts (see Figure 8.2). However, these dollars dropped sharply in 2009 and will fall in future years as both the federal and provincial contributions also drop.

Figure 8.2
Capital Available for Housing

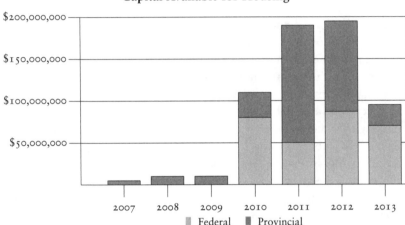

Since the provincial government gutted provincial housing funding and cut policy staff at the housing ministry starting in 1995, the capacity of the Ontario government to effectively design and deliver affordable housing initiatives has been critically eroded.

Ontario did launch one major new housing finance initiative in 2008, when it created a $500-million affordable housing loan fund as part of Infrastructure Ontario.[11] However, over the following two years less than 30 per cent of the available funding – $148.1 million – had actually been allocated.

The Housing Network of Ontario, after its own province-wide consultation, has set out the key elements of a comprehensive and fully funded provincial housing strategy. These elements include, most basically, the construction of more new affordable housing, which would reduce poverty while boosting the economy. In addition, the province's stock of aging affordable housing units needs to be refurbished, and the programs introduced by various levels of government need to be better co-ordinated.

Some of the proposals submitted by HNO partners are tried and true housing initiatives: capital funding to get new homes built; a universal housing benefit to ensure that the housing remains affordable to low-

and moderate-income households; funding for repairs and social supports. The group also supported initiatives that are new for Ontario, such as an inclusionary housing policy that would require that affordable homes be a part of *every* new housing development, including those being built by private developers. A very useful initiative would be a tax credit to assist low- and modest-income households in the purchase of their own homes.

After the formal consultations ended in December, the HNO pulled together the most important overall proposals into its tests for success for Ontario's long-term affordable housing strategy.[12] These include the need for bold targets and multi-year funding of high-quality, affordable housing for Ontarians to include a minimum of ten thousand universally accessible affordable non-profit and co-op developed housing units annually over ten years. At least half of those need to be "rent geared to income." Moreover, as any homeowner knows, housing needs maintenance. So Ontario needs an annualized fund to repair and maintain both existing housing and the new units. Because land costs are a crucial element of any housing development, government needs to make public land available for affordable housing while creating innovative financing options for developers of affordable housing. Finally, the province needs to recapture the expertise in non-profit housing development that was frittered away after 1995. We need to strengthen the development and technical capacity of the affordable housing sector.

The Ontario government has made much of its Poverty Reduction Strategy. This strategy, quite correctly, includes long-term commitments. These are backed up by "targets and measures," reflecting one of the most popular concepts of our era – accountability. The HNO's affordable housing strategy reflects this approach. It includes a solid measuring stick to provide not only accurate evidence about the scale of housing insecurity and homelessness in Ontario but also a clear means of measuring progress. The evaluation needs to determine whether Ontario is systematically reducing the number of households on affordable housing waiting lists across the province. A key target is a consistent annual reduction in the proportion of Ontario tenants spending more than 30 per cent of their income on housing. We also need to improve access to suitable affordable housing for marginalized groups, including Aboriginal people, communities of colour, people with disabilities and mental health issues, lone mothers, and people living in rural and Northern communities. Finally, Ontario has far too many people living in homeless shelters, and far too many others living in fear of eviction due to high rental costs. Their numbers must be consistently reduced.

With respect to accountability, a basic principle is that those affected by decisions should have a say in making those decisions. The HNO has emphasized the need for annual public reporting on progress and a commitment to ongoing public consultation. New housing programs should feature local control of program design and delivery. This needs to be accomplished by nurturing residents review committees that would be equitably representative of people who have experienced housing insecurity. Finally, Ontario is sorely in need of improved co-ordination of housing and related programs between ministries. One priority is the appointment of a full-time minister of housing to ensure that affordable housing remains a government priority.

All Ontarians need housing that they can afford. To this end, HNO has proposed a monthly universal housing benefit for low-income Ontarians aimed at closing the gap between low incomes and high housing costs. We also need to expand the social housing priority list to include Aboriginal people, communities of colour, people with disabilities and mental health issues, lone mothers, and others facing discrimination by landlords. Retrofitting of existing housing stock should ensure that older units are accessible for people with disabilities. As far as new housing is concerned, Ontario needs at least two thousand new supportive housing units annually to provide services to allow people with disabilities, mental health issues, and addictions to maintain their housing.

Finally, existing legislation has a profound effect on affordable housing and the ways in which our communities take shape. Laws governing municipal planning, social housing, and the private rental market must be reformed to promote growth in affordable housing, better protect the housing rights of tenants, and provide flexibility for non-profit and co-operative housing providers. The *Social Housing Reform Act* needs to be amended to give community housing providers control and a fair appeals process to review decisions made by service managers. We can improve fairness by restricting punitive rent-geared-to-income rules and allowing tenants the right to independent review of loss-of-subsidy decisions. The *Residential Tenancies Act* needs to be changed to better protect tenants and to ensure that landlords cannot raise rents on vacant units beyond rent regulation guidelines. The *Planning Act* can be improved by allowing municipalities to introduce inclusionary housing policies to create new affordable housing. Cities also need the power to expropriate abandoned properties for affordable housing conversion.

In 1995 the government of the day, in the course of its frontal assault on public provision for our most vulnerable neighbours, justified the wholesale dismantling of housing funding and programs by announcing that Ontario was "getting out of the housing business." While a new government was elected in 2003 with the promise of ramping up provincial housing initiatives, Ontario has remained at the bottom of the pack on housing initiatives over most of the past two decades.

It was simple enough to quickly destroy Ontario's affordable housing infrastructure. It will be more complex – and it will take longer – to rebuild both the affordable housing stock and the development infrastructure necessary to do the job. The provincial government of 2010 organized a massive public consultation on affordable housing. The message was loud and clear. The time is ripe. The stage is set. Before and after the provincial election of 2011 Ontario will be judged by just how well it heeds this message.

9

The Cost of Hunger:
Food Security and Health Issues

"You know that commercial on TV, where a person opens a can of food and their house disappears? It's like that."
– Participant, Waterloo, describes having to choose between paying for shelter or food

B ALANCING A FOOD HAMPER ON HER HIP, Suzanne reaches out to ring the door bell of an old brick house in Halton. Donna, an elderly woman, appears at the door, grateful that her weekly food delivery has arrived. Due to her age, Donna has trouble getting around, and Suzanne kindly volunteers her time to deliver food each week.

Suzanne delivers food hampers to twenty-four families on a weekly basis. She covers the cost of the transportation herself. "I am helping people who can't come and get the food themselves," she says matter of factly.

Unbeknownst to those who benefit from her generosity, Suzanne understands all too well the struggle to buy and transport nutritious and healthy food on a low income. Suzanne has been receiving help from the Ontario Disability Support Program for seven months, and she received Ontario Works for five years before that. She attended the Halton audit to support her friend, Jocelyn, and ended up sharing her own stories.

Years before, Suzanne was working as a subcontractor for a large company when she learned she was pregnant. She was not able to continue working in the construction business while she was pregnant. At the time of the audit she was living in Acton with her two children, ages six and eight. In Acton a two-bedroom apartment costs at least $500 per month, and the grocery store closest to her often had high prices. There were more reasonably priced supermarkets in nearby Georgetown, but she could not afford to drive there.

"It would be nice if there was affordable anything," she told us. "If it wasn't for affordable housing, most of us would be on the streets."

Suzanne was relying heavily on food banks to provide for herself and her two young children. She often had to ration the food to make it last. A can of soup typically feeds one person, but Suzanne had to split the contents between both of her children. Sometimes she was unable to eat because there was not enough food.

"First priority is children, adults come second. If I have to eat bread and butter so my kids can eat better, that is what I have to do."

Participants at the York audit shared countless stories about the economic and physical inaccessibility of nutritious, healthy food. After they paid for their rent, utilities, and medications, they had precious little of an OW or ODSP cheque left over for food. Some participants at the York audit reported picking through garbage, searching for morsels they could salvage.

"I thought that garbage-picking was only needed in the Philippines, Africa, and other third world countries," a rapporteur commented at the audit. "I cannot imagine it happening right in Ontario, one of the richest provinces of Canada."

"We don't even get enough to have a healthy diet, which contributes to heart disease, health costs, obesity," said Maggie, a participant at the York Region audit. "But that's okay because we are stupid poor people." She paused. "I'm being facetious."

The World Food Summit of 1996 defined food security as being "when all people, at all times, have physical and economic access to sufficient, safe, and nutritious food to meet their dietary needs and food preferences for an active and healthy life." The Government of Canada and Dieticians of Canada have adopted this definition.[1] Food security is a social determinant of health (see chapter 12). Where food *insecurity* exists, a person's physical, mental, and emotional health is severely damaged, sometimes irreparably. Food security and insecurity occur on multiple levels: individual, family or household, community, and national. The stories gathered at the social audits told of the experiences in this regard, on both a personal and community scale, of countless low-income people.

Food Banks Canada's *Hunger Report 2009* revealed that 794,738 individuals across the country had received help from a food bank or affiliated food program in one month – March 2009 – alone.[2] Food programs affiliated with food banks include soup kitchens, school meal programs, shelters, or other community resources. The figure of 794,738 for one month represents the largest year-to-year increase on record – a growth of a full 18 per cent in comparison to the same period in 2008. About one-third of these individuals were children.

Ontario experienced the third-highest increase in food bank usage in the country, rising by 19 per cent in 2009. Food banks in Ontario served 56,250 more individuals in 2009 than they did in 2008. In March 2009 across Canada, 9.1 per cent of food bank users were seeking assistance for the first time.

Just who does use food banks? The answer to this question provides a glimpse of the human face of food insecurity in Canada. Over half – 51.5 per cent – of all food bank users receive income from social assistance. According to Food Banks Canada, 87 per cent of food bank users live in rental accommodations. Of these people, 52 per cent pay market rent and 15 per cent live in social housing. Nearly half of those assisted were families with children, including a fairly even split between two-parent and single-parent families. Some 12 per cent of food bank users were Aboriginal people, even though Aboriginal people make up only 3.8 per cent of Canada's population.[3]

The recent global recession not only contributed to the increased demand placed on food banks in 2009, but also limited the funding and resources that were available to food banks to serve their communities. The *Hunger Report 2009* showed that most food banks are only able to provide several days' worth of food at a time to a client. Over half of all food banks are only able to serve a client once per month. Certain types of food, such as milk, eggs, and meat, are difficult to collect by donation, so food banks often purchase these items. Over half of all food banks reported purchasing more food than usual in order to match demand. Food banks are primarily staffed by volunteers, and 49 per cent of all food banks have no paid staff on hand. In addition to this limited personnel, the *Hunger Report* revealed: "35 per cent of food banks lack adequate, good quality space; 22 per cent lack necessary equipment such as shelving and cold storage; 23 per cent strive, and fail, to recruit enough volunteers to fully manage everyday operations."

Despite being underfunded and volunteer-driven, food banks have become an integral part of Canada's social safety net. How did we get to this point? The recession has undoubtedly played a role in the increased use of food banks, but food insecurity in Canada has been a fact of life, and building, for years. As the *Hunger Report* points out, "Even before the economic downturn, food banks and their affiliated agencies had been assisting more than 700,000 people per month for most of the past decade. This is a status quo that can, and must, change."[4]

The issue of food insecurity, and the shift of responsibility from the state to the voluntary sector to deal with it, has progressed over decades. Notable changes to Canada's social policies took place during the 1990s as a neo-liberal free-market ideology caused the upheaval of any remnants of a Keynesian welfare state. The federal government slashed financial transfers to provinces and territories to fund education, health care, and social services. Hostility and intolerance towards poor people pervaded government policies as eligibility for social assistance was restricted and "harsh and punitive regulations" were imposed on those who received social assistance.[5] In 1995 Ottawa restructured unemployment insurance (now employment insurance), causing fewer workers to be eligible for benefits and limiting the scope of benefits. The federal government also cancelled social housing programs and introduced the recovery (commonly called the "clawback") of the National Child Benefit in some provinces.[6] In 1995 in Ontario social assistance rates were reduced by 21.6 per cent. Some fifteen years later, social assistance rates were still below the level that individuals received prior to the Mike Harris cuts.

All of these factors culminated in an alarmingly high incidence of food insecurity among individuals and families in Ontario and across Canada. Food insecurity is directly tied to income and poverty. The commodification of food has meant that those who are unemployed or live on social assistance simply do not have access to nutritious food. There is not enough money to buy an adequate amount of healthy food.

To truly understand the struggle facing Suzanne, Maggie, and others, we need to crunch the numbers. A single person with no children on Ontario Works receives $585 each month. The average rent for a bachelor apartment in Toronto was $802 in April 2010, up from $772 in April 2009.[7] Without enough money to pay for rent, how can people even begin to manage their budgets for food? Individuals are forced to live in substandard, dangerous, and crowded conditions just to keep a roof over their heads. People are forced to rely on food banks and soup kitchens, all of which are stretched beyond their capacities. Others may turn to food theft as a desperate last resort. Suppose someone lives in a more affordable city in Ontario, such as Kitchener. The average rent for a bachelor apartment in Kitchener was $596 in April 2010, up from $576 in April 2009.[8] A single person on OW in Kitchener has exactly $9 left to pay for food, basic hygiene products, and medication. Forget about transportation, or luxuries such as haircuts and clothing.

So, how do people survive?

While ISARC was leading community hearings across the province in early 2010, the Stop Community Food Centre of Toronto sponsored a "Do the Math Challenge."[9] Ten high-profile Torontonians each lived on a food bank grocery hamper for one week and shared their experiences through blog entries and town hall sessions. Participants included writers Naomi Klein and Wayne Roberts, Toronto city councillor Joe Mihevc, and the Toronto medical officer of health, Dr. David McKeown. Participants rationed their food and found that they had to plan ahead very carefully. There was no room for errors, because errors cost you food. Naomi Klein commented, "What we kept finding is that it doesn't matter how good a cook you are, we didn't have the ingredients for a single recipe."[10] The resulting meals were tasteless and starchy. Breakfast becomes plain oatmeal with a splash of milk (if you have any milk left). Lunch might be cream of mushroom soup and a fried egg. Dinner consists of a casserole made only of elbow macaroni, a can of tomato sauce, and a can of tuna. Don't turn your nose up, because that's what you'll have for lunch tomorrow as well.

Participants tolerated the bland flavours and low nutritional density of the food bank products, but their pantries began to empty before the week's end. A number of participants reported skipping meals to make the food last. To save the small quantity of milk they had been given, Wayne Roberts and his family drank black tea all week. Participants blogged about feeling sluggish, weak, and irritable. Several reported losing weight at an unhealthy rate over the course of the week. Others sought out downtown drop-in centres that offered free meals. This can be a time-consuming process, particularly if you are travelling by foot. Many of the participants did not make it to the end of the one-week challenge, either because they had run out of food or because they could not tolerate the ill health effects associated with malnutrition.

For those receiving ow or odsp, food insecurity is an inescapable reality. The individuals at the social audits planned, rationed, begged, and walked long distances to find free meals. How can you be expected to have the energy to work, or even to search for work, when you are struggling to keep from fainting due to malnourishment? Or dealing with stomach pains and indigestion due to a high-sodium, high-fat diet, void of fresh vegetables and meat? Not to mention the travel time of searching for the best deals or getting to and from various soup kitchens.

At Martha's Table, a community food program in Kingston, Martin talked about how he was managing to eat with his limited social assistance cheque. He calmly recited the lunch and dinner programs available across town for each day of the week. It became quickly apparent that what he was outlining was how people cope on social assistance. This was Martin's everyday life – and it had been that way for nearly fifteen years. He looked down at the red-and-white-checkered table-cloth, strumming his fingers on the table. His voice perked up slightly as he offered tips on how to get extra bread and salad at one church downtown. He had lost the sense that this was not normal. This way of living, of barely getting by, was his "normal." His entire day could be taken up by travelling to and from different churches and community gathering places, searching for meals. He was in survival mode.

Everyone ISARC spoke to was in survival mode, including Christine, a single mother in Halton. Christine had limited time during her work-day while her young daughter was at school. She did not have the time to travel to different meal programs or to search for deals at supermar-kets. The grocery store closest to her home and workplace was also more expensive.

"It eats up more of my money," she said. "I feed my daughter, then my two cats, then I am last on the list. I am always last on the list."

Eloise, a single, disabled parent of three in Niagara Region, was in a similar situation. She had to plan meals carefully and ration the food she bought. "I have to limit the food they can eat to make sure it lasts to the end of the month. This is painful to me. Children should not have to live this way, and the citizens of Ontario and Welland just do not understand what it means to be on public assistance."

A mother in North Bay was sacrificing her own health and well-being for her children. "If my husband and I want our kids to eat healthy," she explained, "I have to give up my heart medication, stom-ach medication, and migraine medication, and I do it because our kids come first."

People at several audits had ideas – some of which are being imple-mented as part of the rapidly expanding local food security movement – about ways of improving food security and health for low-income peo-ple. Sonjah suggested cooking classes that also teach how to budget and read nutrition labels. She also proposed providing recipes using ingredi-ents available from food banks. Community gardens were suggested as a viable way of providing fresh vegetables in a cost-effective manner to people on low incomes. Participants from several different audits reported planting their own vegetable gardens because they could not afford to buy fresh produce.

Although these ideas may temporarily improve the well-being of those on social assistance, they ultimately do not address the systemic problems that perpetuate food insecurity. *People need more money. Social assistance rates are appallingly low.* It is insulting and absurd to expect anyone to survive on such little income. For a time the government was giving people more money for food, in the form of the Special Diet Allowance, which enabled individuals on social assistance to receive up to $250 extra per month to cover the costs of the healthy diet needed to manage certain health conditions. The Ontario Coalition Against Poverty (OCAP) helped people on social assistance navigate the bureaucracy of applying for the SDA. The combined efforts of OCAP and physicians allowed many low-income people to qualify for the much-needed SDA in order to manage health conditions such as diabetes, obesity, and heart conditions. As costs soared for the SDA, which was largely unknown before OCAP's advocacy work, the government began to clamp down. The Liberal government announced in spring 2010 that the SDA would be scrapped and replaced with a nutritional supplement administered by the Ministry of Health. Only individuals with "severe" health conditions will qualify for the new nutritional supplement.

The true questions to be asked are these: What is the cost of food security? And what is the cost of food *insecurity*?

Since 1974 the government has calculated the cost of a basic healthy diet using the National Nutritious Food Basket. Data is also collected locally to determine the cost of a Nutritious Food Basket (NFB) for major metropolitan centres. The NFB includes basic food staples such as flour and oil, meat, and vegetables, as well as spices and beverages. It does not include hygiene products or cleaning products. In May 2009 the Ottawa Public Health office determined that the cost of a monthly NFB for a family of four in the Ottawa area would be $735.[11] A "family of four" is considered one man and one woman aged thirty-one to fifty, one boy aged fourteen to eighteen, and one girl aged four to eight.

The estimates from Ottawa point out that food costs are higher for smaller groups of people. A single thirty-year-old man would require a monthly budget of $273.60 to afford a basic nutritious diet. Given that the average rent for a bachelor apartment in Ottawa in April 2010 was $688,[12] a basic monthly budget for rent and healthy food for a single thirty-year-old man would be $961.60. If this individual was on OW, he would only be receiving $585 per month. Again, these figures only cover rent and basic food. Transportation, household products, personal hygiene items, clothing, and school supplies are additional.

Increasing social assistance rates and introducing a dietary or nutritional supplement would cost Ontario money. Toronto's medical officer of health David McKeown estimates that introducing a $100 Healthy Food Supplement for all adults receiving social assistance – not just those with documented medical issues – would cost the province about $470 million.[13] But what is the cost if we do not act? What is the cost to the public health system if individuals on social assistance remain desperately malnourished?

As demonstrated by the Do the Math campaign, even one week of eating the high-sodium, low-nutrient foods from a grocery hamper can seriously undermine a person's health. It is not healthy for people to subsist on plain pasta and cans of tuna. A poor diet is undeniably linked to heart disease, obesity, diabetes, high blood pressure and cholesterol, and many more health issues. According to McKeown, increasing the social assistance rates and introducing a basic Healthy Food Supplement for all adults on social assistance will stimulate the economy in the short term and reduce the incidence of health issues, relieving strain on the public health system.

Pay now. Or pay more, sooner than later.

10 Food Insecurity: A Source of Suffering and Ill Health

Elaine Power

> We will implement policies aimed at eradicating poverty and inequality and improving physical and economic access by all, at all times, to sufficient, *nutritionally* adequate and safe food.
>
> — Commitment of Canadian government,
> Declaration on World Food Security, 1996

> When my daughter came up to me and said "Mummy, I'm hungry and I want a snack," I felt like crying. I wanted to cry. Because I knew I didn't have any extra food.
>
> — Single mother living on social assistance, Toronto

"LET'S EAT!"

We gather to share food. Mealtimes mean togetherness as we participate in the rituals of "breaking bread" – a ritual that symbolizes belonging.

Food is also, of course, a basic biological need. It is required on a daily basis in adequate quality and quantity to maintain life and health. Food has been repeatedly recognized as a basic human right, enshrined in international covenants such as the Universal Declaration of Human Rights. And beyond the biological, what we eat is deeply personal. It reflects our tastes and traditions. Food thus has multiple layers of meaning, filling social and physical needs and generating a sense of self-respect and dignity.

But for Ontarians struggling to eat on low incomes, food's layers of meaning are often flipped upside down. The very necessity of having to make a choice between paying various household bills and buying groceries actually strips away dignity and self-respect. Instead it generates worry and stress. Being unable to buy the types of food that you prefer erodes your sense of belonging in a consumer society in which "choice" reigns supreme. Being forced to face a lineup in a food bank or to depend on the offerings of a soup kitchen is demoralizing. Mental, emotional, nutritional, and physical health all suffer.

The grocery bill is one of the few expenses over which low-income households have some direct control. Rent is a fixed cost. You have to pay for hydro and heat, or get cut off. Yet you can cut back on the quality and, to some extent, the quantity of food when other bills take priority. In 2004, while the economy was still expanding, 8.4 per cent of Ontario households were worried about how they were going to feed themselves and their families.[1] These households would have used a myriad of strategies to manage their tight resources to stave off hunger.[2] They compromised the quality of food that they ate, perhaps substituting hot dogs for better quality meat. They bought cheap, filling foods such as bread and potatoes rather than fresh fruit and vegetables, which are more nutritious but cost much more per calorie. They bought cheap margarine rather than butter. Some families had relatives who could help them out with food; others borrowed money, cut services such as cable, or pawned their possessions.

In about a third of food-insecure households, family members skipped meals and went hungry. In households with children, most often it is the mothers who do not eat so that their children and husbands can. Despite parents' best efforts to juggle slim resources, in some families children actually miss school because the food available – perhaps a bread, margarine, and sugar sandwich – is embarrassing to eat in a public place like school. Sometimes children simply go hungry. Nationally, among households with children, 5.2 per cent of parents reported that in the previous year their children ate poor quality food or did not have enough to eat because of lack of money.[3]

The level of food insecurity in Canada remains appallingly high despite the expansion and institutionalization of food banks. The appearance of food banks in Canada in the early 1980s was one of the first signs of the deterioration of our collective social safety net. Although the number of food banks, and the number of Canadians using them, has risen dramatically over the past quarter-century, food banks do not and cannot solve the problem of hunger and food insecurity. For a variety of reasons, only about a quarter of food-insecure households use food banks.[4] No matter how well intentioned or kind, charity, by its nature, is always stigmatizing, demeaning, and demoralizing for its recipients.[5] Not surprisingly, about 40 per cent of the recipients of food from food banks are children, because parents will do almost anything to keep their children from going hungry (even though many parents can't bring themselves to tell their kids that the food in the cupboard is from the food bank). Many adults would rather go hungry than "stoop" to using the services of food banks; it is a symbol of hitting bottom. Others, perhaps attempting to preserve their own dignity, prefer to leave the food at the food bank for those whom they consider to be "worse off."

Moreover, food banks are clearly limited. Because they depend on donations and volunteer labour, food banks can only provide what they have on hand. Their stock is strictly rationed and controlled, with limits on the amount of food given out at any one time (usually two to three days' worth) and how often households can receive food (often only once a month). Many food banks do their best to accommodate personal preferences and dietary restrictions as well as religious and cultural constraints, but they are often unable to do.

The inadequacy of food banks became all the more obvious in 2009 in the face of the worst economic downturn since the Great Depression. That year demand for food bank services soared in the largest year over year increase on record.[6] Ontario was one of the hardest hit, with a 19 per cent increase in demand compared to 2008. We do not yet have the data to know how these figures correspond with objective measures of how many Ontarians are actually experiencing food insecurity. It does seem likely, though, that with unemployment rates persistently high, and workers' employment benefits running out, our patchwork reliance on a system of charitable food banks to meet the food needs of low-income Ontarians will become even more glaringly inadequate. More people will turn to help that is not there.

□

People are food insecure because they are poor, and in Ontario being on social assistance guarantees poverty. Since the peak of Ontario social assistance rates in 1992, the real amount that recipients receive (in constant dollars) has declined by up to 36 per cent.[7] The biggest hit to rates came with the 21.6 per cent cut that the Conservative government under Mike Harris made shortly after it was elected in 1995; however, under Premier Dalton McGuinty the provincial Liberal government has done little to reverse the decline. This is especially true for the category of "single person considered employable," whose income in 2008 was 40 per cent of the after-tax low-income cut-off (LICO), Canada's primary measure of poverty; 45 per cent of the market basket measure; and 22 per cent of the after-tax average income.[8]

The provincial government's own data, collected by its public health units every year using a tool called the Nutritious Food Basket, confirm the impossibility of eating a basic, nutritious diet on social assistance. For example, in Kingston, where I live, a bachelor apartment cost an average of $586 per month in 2009 – or 99 per cent of the monthly income of a single person on Ontario Works. This left $6 per month for all other expenses. Considering that Kingston, Frontenac and Lennox and Addington Public Health calculates that it would cost $239 per month for a male of age thirty-one to fifty to eat a basic, healthy diet, it is clear that OW rates inflict malnutrition among recipients.[9]

Not surprisingly, then, the spotlight of anti-poverty advocacy and activism over the past few years has turned to food. In February 2005 the Ontario Coalition Against Poverty seized on the Special Diet Allowance program to enable social assistance recipients to get access to extra money for food, up to $250 a month. The SDA was set up by the Ministry of Community and Social Services for eligible social assistance recipients to cover the extra costs incurred in eating a medically pre-scribed diet associated with a health condition. To get access to the SDA, the social assistance recipient had to ask a health-care provider to fill out a form, and then present that form to his or her caseworker.

Until November 2005 the SDA could be paid out for either a speci-fied medical condition, such as diabetes, or for a specific diet type, such as a "high protein, high calorie" diet required for weight gain. Reason-ably enough, OCAP argued that because social assistance rates are inade-quate to cover the costs of a healthy diet, all social assistance recipients are de facto malnourished and should be eligible for the SDA. Clinics were set up in cities across the province, with sympathetic health-care providers signing up thousands of social assistance recipients for the Special Diet Allowance.

As the cost of the SDA program began to climb (by an extra $40 million in 2005), the Ministry of Community and Social Services clamped down. In November 2005 a new, more restrictive application form was put into place that no longer listed particular diets, but only medical conditions. The Ministry also announced a review of all SDA cases, requiring that recipients provide information about any medical conditions that necessitated a special diet. Those receiving the SDA who did not have a medical condition as specified on the new form were cut off.

In June 2006 the Ministry formed an SDA Expert Review Commit-tee, with the mandate of advising the government about which medical conditions warrant a special diet and the extraordinary costs of those special diets. The Committee's final report, released in April 2008, made a highly questionable assumption: *"that the amount provided to Ontario Works and Ontario Disability Support Recipients for basic needs was sufficient to purchase the minimum Food Guide Servings outlined in Canada's Food Guide."*[10]

The reasoning was that the SDA was meant to provide a "top-up" so that adequately nourished social assistance recipients who have a medical condition requiring additional or special (more expensive) foods can afford to treat their medical condition. The patent absurdity of this assumption, as demonstrated by the Ontario Public Health Units' Nutritious Food Basket calculations, led to the early resignation of three of the original members of the Expert Review Committee, myself included. The Ontario Public Health Association lodged a formal protest after the release of the final report.[11]

The bulk of the Committee's report consisted of fairly dry and detailed calculations of the costs of special diets such as those for celiac disease, kidney disease, childhood growth failure, high blood pressure, high cholesterol, and several other medical conditions, with special consideration for costs in Northern Ontario. The figures presented are illuminating. Consider the "extra" food costs of a diagnosis of diabetes, one of many diseases that are more common among the poor than among those who are wealthier. According to the Expert Review Committee, people diagnosed with diabetes should be spending, on average, an *extra $89.58 per month* (adjusted for inflation to 2009 dollars) on top of the regular food budget to meet their dietary prescriptions. Diet is a well-recognized cornerstone of diabetes management. For anyone with this illness, the lack of a proper diet means that further health problems are likely.

Take our standardized case study of the single man living on Ontario Works in Kingston. It this man were to be diagnosed with diabetes – and if he was not signed up for the Special Diet Allowance (and many are not) – the additional expense of following his prescribed diabetic diet would bring his theoretical food costs to 55.5 per cent of his monthly social assistance income. A weight loss diet for obesity, another common medical condition, would cost an estimated additional $56.04 per month (in 2009 dollars) in groceries.

The recommendations of the Expert Review Committee were never implemented. Instead, in the wake of an Ontario Human Rights Tribunal decision that would have forced the expansion of the program, the McGuinty government cancelled the program altogether in its March 2010 budget. The government cited the soaring costs of the SDA

program, from $6 million in 2003 to $200 million in 2008, with about
20 per cent of social assistance recipients enrolled in the program.[12]
Given higher rates of all forms of illness among those who are poor, it is
not unreasonable that 20 per cent of social assistance recipients would
be eligible for the SDA. However, instead of seeing the money as an
investment in preventive health for those members of our society who
are most likely to be sick and to die premature deaths, the government
pointed to the 2009 Auditor General's report and insinuated that the
rising costs were due to fraud. In its 2010 budget, the government also
announced that the SDA would be replaced by a new nutritional supplementation program, run by the Ministry of Health and Long-Term
Care. For months thereafter the government failed to provide details of
this proposed program.

Anti-poverty activists were justifiably outraged at the cancellation of
the SDA and worried that the new nutritional supplementation program
would be a cost-cutting measure that excluded many who were previously benefiting from the SDA. The Registered Nurses' Association of
Ontario and the 25 in 5 Network for Poverty Reduction mounted an
advocacy campaign calling on the provincial government to ensure that
the new program adopts five specific principles: 1) people with additional health-related dietary costs will get the financial support they
need; 2) accessibility, adequacy, and equity; 3) the provision of at least
the same amount of money for the new program; 4) an assurance that
current SDA recipients will be no worse off; and 5) establishment of a
well-developed program that is not rushed in its conceptualization and
implementation.[13]

OCAP's Special Diet Allowance campaign was not the only provincial food-related anti-poverty advocacy underway. Early in 2009 a
coalition including the Association of Local Public Health Agencies,
Social Planning Council of Ontario, and 25 in 5 Network for Poverty
Reduction began a campaign, "Put Food in the Budget," calling for an
immediate $100 per month healthy food allowance for all social assis-
tance recipients.[14] Recognizing that this $100 would not be enough to
enable all Ontario Works and Ontario Disability Support Program
recipients to eat a healthy diet, the Coalition called on the government
to implement the allowance immediately to serve as a "downpayment"
and stop-gap measure until the recommendations of the promised full
social assistance review are implemented. As Toronto's Medical Officer
of Health, Dr. David McKeown, argued, the cost of the supplement to
the provincial treasury is an investment that will be paid back not only
in the short term by the local economic boost, but also in the longer

term by the reduced burden of illness due to poor nutrition and poverty.[15]

□

Imagine an Ontario in which no one has to go to bed hungry, rely on food banks for something to eat, tell their children that the food is all gone, or make a choice between heating or eating. Imagine the energy that low-income people might have, the activities they might take up, and the contributions they might make to society if they were properly nourished and no longer worn down by the stress and strain of worrying about where the next meal is coming from. Imagine harnessing all the energy of thousands and thousands of food bank volunteers for other worthy projects. Imagine the savings to the health-care system that would come about if there were an investment in preventive health that ensured that everyone could afford a healthy diet.

Social assistance rates now bear no resemblance to the cost of living. If there were ever a rationale for the levels at which those rates are set, it is lost in the mists of history.

We have the data to set up a market basket approach to social assistance rates that would be tied to the cost of living in different communities around the province. We might quibble about the details of what needs to be included in that market basket to promote dignity and a sense of belonging, but everyone would agree that it has to include access to a basic, healthy diet. The Nutritious Food Basket methodology, developed by Health Canada many years ago, is a respected, useful way of assessing the cost of a basic nutritious diet. The government has already mandated that Public Health Units use the Nutritious Food Basket to collect data annually about the actual cost of a healthy diet. Why does the government not use those data to inform social assistance rates?

As part of its commitment to reduce poverty by 25 per cent by 2013, the Ontario government has promised a full review of the income security system. It is time to ensure that this review is set up. Once it is set up, it will be time to press for social assistance rates that are tied to the real cost of living, including the cost of food. This step would represent an investment in health. It would be an investment in promoting dignity. It would be an investment in the future of the province.

11

Poverty and Health:
"I'm One Stumble from the Street"

Being rich gets a man 11 more years of healthy living.
— *The Globe and Mail*, headline, Nov. 25, 2009

A S A LONG-TIME CLERICAL WORKER for Niagara's regional Community Care Access Centre, Sherene was familiar with how home care was organized to help patients discharged from hospital and other disabled people. She was making a decent wage, $17 dollars an hour. She did not think that she would need home care, at least until well after retirement.

In her early fifties, Sherene had a major stroke of bad luck. A recently licensed seventeen-year-old driver rear-ended her car at high speed, resulting in torn muscles, ligaments, and tendons in her shoulders and back. Some ten years and hundreds of medical and physiotherapy appointments later, she was still struggling with anxiety and depression. For her it was a daunting effort to make her way to Sanatorium Road and the Chedoke Chronic Pain Management Unit.

When she attended the Niagara social audit, Sherene told the story of an ordinary life shattered by sudden misfortune. She had grown up in the Niagara Region, the daughter of working-class parents. They took pride in their independence, and in their ability to provide piano and dance lessons for their daughter.

"My family was self-sufficient," she recalled fondly. "We never received financial help."

Sherene gamely tried to keep working after the accident, holding onto both her job and her post-retirement travel plans until she was finally forced by her disability to leave work. During that time her partner of twenty-one years and several other loved ones died. The pain and loss meant a downward spiral of depression. Although she had paid into the employment insurance system for years, she missed the application deadline and had to watch as her savings dwindled. She told us that she was not eligible for the Ontario Disability Support Program until she had less than $5,000 left.

Hers is a story of loss: loss of work, health, income, and companionship. Recounting that story, Sherene seemed frequently on the verge of tears. She could not afford a car to get to her appointments and was managing on a tight food budget. She declared in a matter-of-fact way that she used the food bank as infrequently as possible because she believed that others needed help more than she did. She now found herself in the position of getting help from the agency for which she once worked.

Eating healthy food had become impossible. Sherene had come to realize that the supply of social housing that would lower her rent costs was far from adequate. Above all, she said, she was frightened. "I'm one stumble from the street."

Ontario's Niagara peninsula was once home to dozens of factories and mills that sprang up along the Welland Canal and took advantage of cheap hydro power from the stately Adam Beck generating station just downstream from Niagara Falls. The area provided a solid base of industrial jobs – everything from boxboard and automotive parts manufacturing to nickel refining and paper mills. Many of the jobs were unionized. With the hollowing out of Southern Ontario's manufacturing base, those days are gone. But abundant wealth remains in a region that is home to flourishing tourism and wine industries. Affluent couples take $800-a-day tours featuring luxurious boutique hotels, sumptuous dining, and private wine-tastings. Global corporations book group tours for clients and employees. This wealth, however, does not trickle down to local people struggling with the challenges of poor health and disability.

Esther, a sole-support mother who lives in the Niagara Region with her twin teenage girls, was born forty years ago with a club foot. When she became pregnant at age nineteen she developed diabetes and had to go on insulin. Yet she cobbled together a living from Mother's Allowance, a part-time job with an employer who took her illness into account, and a lot of babysitting work on the side.

Her twins were born in 1995, just as Ontario's social assistance system was gutted by the poor-bashing of the so-called Common Sense Revolution. She was nevertheless able to rely on a tight social network.

"Thank goodness my family was there to support me," she told the social audit rapporteurs. "They would look after the kids when I got sick."

Esther's health problems began to escalate. Her on-again off-again illnesses, which included osteoarthritis along with diabetes and pain from her long-standing foot ailment, made it harder to find regular work. She then moved back home to look after her ailing mother. She said she "became very depressed and began to take medication," and around that time her disability application was finally accepted.

"Food is still always an issue for me," she told us. She was going "to the soup kitchen" to get food for herself, which meant that she could manage to buy a small amount of food and send it to school for the kids' lunches. "After I pay the rent I have about $400 a month to live on. That might sound like a lot, but it's not. I have to pay for all my transportation and I get money for a diabetic supplement, but I always have to buy more syringes than what is covered in a month. I have a hard time meeting my basic needs."

For her, commonplace items that most people take for granted loomed as huge obstacles. Necessities became huge treats for Esther.

"I went for my first haircut in a year last month, but now spring is here and my one daughter doesn't have any shoes. It's that kind of thing that is tough. Other kids in her class can just go out and buy shoes. Us, we have to plan and save for it. My daughter will have to wait a few weeks until I get my cheque before she can get shoes."

Esther experienced bouts of severe depression that were compounded by her physical problems. She explained that when she was at the hospital – "Thank goodness!" – her landlord would look in on her teenagers.

Just two weeks before she spoke to us she was hospitalized again when her sugar levels shot way up. "My kids are fifteen now and they kind of seem used to me getting sick all the time. . . . It's so hard for everyone to understand. . . . I really just want my kids to stay in school so they don't end up like me."

☐

This reality – being "one stumble from the street" or having to seek out charity meals so your children are able to take a lunch to school – gnaws at a person's self-esteem, the sense of self-worth, particularly in a society that places so much emphasis on what kind of stuff you have. It is not just about *self*-esteem. It is also about how you feel respected and valued – or devalued and disrespected – in the eyes of others. Feelings of insecurity and inferiority are huge causes of stress. One of the things that became abundantly clear in our social audit is that the most vulnerable among us lead chaotic, highly stressful lives. Stress, particularly chronic stress, is a major cause of cardiovascular disease and immune deficiency diseases. These deadly disorders are experienced disproportionately by poor people.

These are not simply impressions gathered in discussions with hundreds of low-income Ontario people. They are now well-established epidemiological facts. But they run contrary to convention wisdom. Many of us still believe that it is the busy CEO and the harried boss, those at the top of the institutional pyramids that dominate our society, who lead the most stressful lives.

Wrong. Breakthrough research that began a generation ago showed that people at the bottom of one particular social hierarchy were three times more likely to die prematurely than were those at the top. Scientists established this finding in a massive study of over ten thousand English civil servants – the now famous Whitehall Study. They pinpointed the key issue, or variable, as the degree of control over one's work. The lower you are on the pyramid, the less control you have over your life, the more stress you are under, and the more likely you are to suffer from coronary heart disease.[1] The lead Whitehall Study scientist, Dr. Michael Marmot, went on to head the landmark 2008 World Health Organization study *Closing the Gap in a Generation: Health Equity through Action on the Social Determinants of Health*. That study explained pointedly: "Social and economic policies have a determining impact on whether a child can grow and develop to its full potential and live a flourishing life, or whether its life will be blighted."[2]

The social audit heard a lot about stress. One witness in Cornwall described what have come to be known in Ontario as the "stupid rules" that govern the social assistance system and the lives of those who depend on it.

"You always have to prove, prove, prove. And the documents required cost money. And that money comes out of my pocket. Out of my budget."

One can only imagine the emotional effects when those official letters arrive – as they so frequently do – threatening to reduce or remove benefits that are already inadequate. A woman trying to supplement her disability assistance by working at home told the Simcoe County social audit: "It is very stressful. When service workers call me sometimes [I] go into 'panic mode.' I have been diagnosed with clinical depression. I am always frightened they will decrease my funding because I am self-employed. They cut back on my funds so much one time that I didn't eat for a week and I fainted while working with a client."

A man in York Region suffering from Type 2 diabetes reflected on his quality of life, pinpointing the issues of stress and control that are front and centre in the social determinants of health research. "I wish I could handle the stress at my age. I don't have any control over others except myself. If I can start eating a bit better and having a couple of dollars in my pocket at the end of the month after my bills are paid, I would probably be more confident mentally and physically. I'd have serenity, peace of mind, and tranquility, and this is the basis of mental health. I'd be a happy camper."

Type 2 diabetes is a disease that has reached epidemic proportions, particularly in poor neighbourhoods. It costs Ontario's health-care system untold millions each year. The Niagara Region social audit report described a poignant situation that reveals how problems such as poor health, poverty, obesity, and stress – along with guilt and sadness – are so tightly interrelated:

"Joyce diagnosed as diabetic recently. Cannot afford medication, nor proper diet. Doctor gives her sample medication. When she is stressed, she eats. Doctor has warned her to lose weight before her next appointment. Had a sinus infection but could not afford medication. Doctor again is good and gives her samples. She is so sad as she could not afford medication when her son was ill, and now her son has a hearing problem in his right ear . . . actually stone deaf. Mother feels very guilty and she could not afford to take her child to the doctor."

The introduction to York Region's comprehensive audit described the way in which the organizers had decided to organize the tremendous amount of material that they received. They "put the themes and elements from these stories within a broader framework of the Determinants of Health . . . [the] risk and protective factors that exist in every facet of people's lives, that increase or threaten their potential for health and wellbeing."

The York Region organizers looked up Health Canada's "determinants of health" and learned that they include income and social status [that is, money and self-esteem], employment, education, child development, gender, and support networks. They met with several people who highlighted the ways in which stress affects their lives.

"I wear a hat constantly because I'm getting bald spots because of stress," said a single mother of two.

"I'm in constant stress – fear of where my next rent money and food money are going to come from," said a man on disability benefits.

Maggie, a mother of two, said, "I have worked all my life. Sitting at home and watching the wall is killing me. I have had anxiety attacks so many times."

Children living in poor families, experiencing stress from an early age – even in utero – are more likely to suffer from stress-related diseases such as stroke, heart disease, and diabetes. With parents facing acute adversity and accompanying anxiety, their prospects do indeed become blighted. One of the Barrie rapporteurs explained: "Poverty causes poor health – and poor health can lead to poverty. The challenge for many is to overcome a downward cycling of illness and financial loss. These dynamics were clearly demonstrated in the testimonials from the four participants in the ISARC social audit that I heard today."

☐

As the World Health Organization reported in 2008, public policies do a lot to determine whether children flourish or endure blighted lives. In 2010 a senior researcher for Statistics Canada reported the results of an investigation into the links between low income, lack of work, and poor health.

Myriam Fortin's data revealed that Canadians who are poor or underemployed have far worse health than most other Canadians do. She wrote that "persistent poverty leads to poor health." She also pointed to something that others have noticed. It might be called the pay-now-or-pay-later dynamic. Noting that health budgets are steadily rising even though governments face large deficits, Fortin concludes, "Investing in the social determinants of health . . . makes sense given the current economic context, where individuals who are otherwise healthy could end up losing their jobs because of the recession which, in turn, might lead them to periods of poverty, and if the situation persists deterioration in health."[3]

Our social audit found out what many others, including former Senator Michael Kirby, have long insisted was a huge problem for people facing mental health challenges and indeed for the overall health-care system. Just as our audit was drawing to a close, Kirby, as chair of the Mental Health Commission of Canada, told a Vancouver conference on Health of the Homeless, "Mental health and addiction represent roughly 35 per cent of the disease burden in Canada, yet these illnesses receive only about 5 per cent of the resources." He argued that this imbalance costs taxpayers dearly and shifts treatments from other health-care needs.[4]

The story of Frank from North Bay illustrates how the short-term, band-aid approach to poverty and mental health leads to higher long-term costs.

"I have no motivation, no self-confidence. It has such a big impact on [my] self-esteem, confidence, not to be able to do simple things like brush your teeth or take a shower. There isn't even enough money for simple things like toothpaste and soap. I am entirely capable of functioning on my own but I just don't have the resources to live independently. This severely affects my mental health."

Later that day the Community Living support worker who had accompanied Frank to the social audit attended one of our focus groups for front-line workers. Paulette was blunt about the vicious circle of poverty and poor health that so many people confront every day.

"Their mental health needs are so great now because they've been stuck in this poverty cycle for so long that they've spiralled downwards and are less confident and able than they used to be. We [their helpers] are overwhelmed by their basic needs. This could have been prevented by some earlier support."

Pay now or pay – more – later. It was a recurring theme in the social audit. Another North Bay service provider explained the frustration of her struggle to get her clients the dental care they so desperately need in our reactive system of care: "Since January 2010, the dental program CINOT [Children in Need of Treatment] has expanded to include emergency treatment for kids up to seventeen. We have many who need treatment, but it is difficult to find dentists willing to accept our referral clients. We hear from many desperate adults who need dental treatment, but can't afford it. They end up in the hospital ER, where the cost to treat an acute infection is so very expensive compared to the cost for preventative maintenance."

One of the great tragedies faced by people living in poverty is their inability to afford even the most basic dental care. Their teeth rot in their mouths because the commercial marketplace continues to dominate the dental care system nearly a half century after public health care came to Canada – even though it is well established that poor dental health is linked to a decline in both physical and mental health. It's as if our mouths are not connected to the rest of our bodies.

A mother, married with two children, told the Niagara social audit that she had not seen a dentist since before her children were born. She had no dental coverage and could not afford to pay for a visit to the dentist. Her own dental problems were being left untreated, and her children had never been to the dentist.

In North Bay we heard about the dental problems faced by people on disability benefits. A woman described substandard dental care: "I finally found a dentist who would take me as an ODSP client. He took twenty minutes to fill six cavities. If I had a [private] plan I think he'd take twenty minutes to fill just one cavity. They won't give you the same care. The work I've had done is substandard."

While people on social assistance do qualify for rudimentary dental care, things are different for those in marginal and low-wage jobs.

"Dental care is a major concern for me and my husband," said a woman from Markham. "I used to work in the head office of Shoppers Drug Mart, and I had coverage [then]. Lately my fillings are falling out and my teeth have decay. My husband has stubs for teeth. If we were on ODSP or OW we might get help. Since we are the working poor we don't get anything. We might have to die because we cannot afford this care. Dental care should be universal like OHIP. It's a basic health-care right."

Another woman, who does get some basic dental coverage from ODSP, said that she was going to the community college for cleaning and assessment. "I feel like a second-class citizen."

□

In small towns the stress and stigma of poverty are magnified because everyone knows you are poor. One woman, Jill, told us about the time when she was approached on the street by a well-meaning lady who saw her and noticed that Jill was wearing her old, discarded clothes.

"The poor are not uneducated or unmotivated," observed a rapporteur at the Mountain social audit. "From what I witnessed these are men and women who have more strength, courage, and resolve than most. They are survivors [who] have to fight for everything they receive while at the same time trying to keep their dignity and respect. But when someone is fighting for so long, one begins to feel beaten to the point of brokenness."

Social justice advocates often point to the bitter choice facing low-income parents: pay the rent or feed the kids. In Mountain the rapporteurs met a man who confronted a variation on this theme.

"Poor health is part of his daily experience. He has to choose between food and medication. A few extra dollars a month for a diabetic diet is not enough for one healthy meal. He shows us his tremor, which can only be controlled with expensive medication. We share a moment of silence which is full of compassion."

Advocates and activists have been working to promote the public good through public health since the nineteenth century. That was when germ theory gave rise to new understandings of how deadly diseases like cholera and typhoid spread. The new understanding that we could act to prevent epidemics gave rise to a new way of thinking called the "sanitary idea." No longer was "bad air" or an imbalance of body "humours" believed to cause sickness. Rather, it was simply a matter of providing the basics of public health – clean water, adequate sewage disposal, pasteurized milk, garbage disposal.

Today's public health advocates also have a new way of thinking. Buoyed by clear epidemiological evidence no less convincing than Louis Pasteur's germ theory, a key aspect of the new thinking is that health and accompanying social problems are more common in countries with higher income inequalities, to the extent that these two factors are "extraordinarily closely related." Canadians find themselves in the middle of the poor health and inequality scale, halfway between healthier and more equal countries such as Japan and Sweden and, at the other end, the United States and Portugal.[5]

In 2008 the first annual report to Parliament from Dr. David Butler-Jones, Canada's new Chief Public Health Officer, pointed to the "good evidence" that several key factors were having a "profound effect" on our health. Those factors include poverty, early childhood development, literacy, decent housing, food security, and social status.[6] The list is remarkably similar to the table of contents of this book.

Public health, as one 2010 headline explained, represents "a voice for the underdog."[7] Our social audit heard from both the underdogs and those committed to helping them make their way through the thorny thickets that they find themselves in, and from which they must escape. Senior staff at Kingston's Community Health Centre explained that poor people never have just one problem. They tend to have more complex health conditions and are at greater risk of secondary and tertiary impact. Often discharged from hospital with no follow-up plan and insufficient money to buy prescriptions, they find it harder to deal with chronic illnesses such as diabetes or high blood pressure. They find it harder to get access to necessary information, good nutrition, and proper support systems. Middle-class people can buy help when they need it. Poor people can't.

Our health system, despite the public provision for primary care, is still weighted towards a market-based supply, the purchase of goods and services. We found that low-income people experience what amounts to a "Yo-Yo" effect, or what seems like someone dangling at the end of a You're-On-Your-Own string. This was the experience of one Cornwall woman. Diagnosed with ovarian cancer, Natalie began to experience recurring migraines after her several surgeries. She was no longer able to work. Her daughter suffered from Attention Deficit Hyperactivity Disorder and diabetes. They had no money for medications not covered by what Natalie called her "Drug Card." She reported that she was being worn down by constantly having to justify her need for assistance.

"I have to pay forty dollars every six months to get a letter saying that, 'Yes, my daughter is diabetic. She still suffers from it and it did not go away.' Every three months I have to bring them a letter confirming that I am unable to work."

After hearing this and so many similar stories, we found it hardly surprising that stress, stigma, and feelings of chronic exclusion are continuing to erode the health of Ontario's low-income people.

12 Poverty Makes Us Sick

Dennis Raphael

> Social injustice is killing people on a grand scale.
> – World Health Organization, *Closing the Gap in a Generation*, 2008

B reaking the Cycle, the title of Ontario's anti-poverty strategy, implies that poverty is a problem rooted in the characteristics and personal failings of certain people. In Ontario some 13 per cent of the population is living in poverty. Can so many people in such a rich province really be poor because of individual failings?

Individual explanations focus on the personal attributes of a number of people and on how these characteristics lead to poverty. According to such explanations, poverty results from a lack of education (on the part of individuals and groups), lack of personal motivation, the presence of physical or mental illness, or intentional dependence on the welfare or social assistance system. They ignore how society is organized in such a way that vulnerable people (those with little education or with a physical or emotional affliction) end up living in poverty.

In the Scandinavian countries of Northern Europe the poverty rate among children is less than 5 per cent, as compared to 15 per cent among Canadian children. Is it reasonable to assume that the parents of Scandinavian children are profoundly more educated, motivated, and lacking in physical or mental illness than their Canadian counterparts are? Clearly, cross-national jurisdictional differences in poverty rates have to be based on more than the presence or absence of various individual characteristics.

Poverty is a prime cause of physical and mental illness. Poverty is a prime cause of social disorder – it creates unsafe, crime-ridden, and fearful neighbourhoods and communities. Finally, poverty threatens our humanity as it renders meaningless not only Canadian values of peace, order, and good government, but also numerous Canadian commitments to uphold international human rights covenants.[1]

Governments faced with these threats are doing little to remedy the situation. Instead of taking lessons from jurisdictions that have acted forcefully to reduce the incidence of poverty, governments, in their inaction, serve to make an already bad situation even worse. The result is a downward spiral in which Canadian well-being – physical, mental, social, and ethical – deteriorates, with weakening expectations that the situation can be reversed.

☐

One important conceptual issue related to poverty concerns the distinction between absolute and relative poverty. Absolute poverty is the inability to have one's basic human needs met. Canadians sleeping on the street or queuing up at food banks, or Aboriginal people living without running water, are illustrations of absolute poverty in Canada.[2]

Relative poverty is the inability to obtain the economic and social resources necessary to engage in behaviours expected of societal members (for example, attending educational, social, or recreational events; maintaining a healthy diet; securing adequate housing; dressing appropriately for the seasons; buying gifts for special occasions). In both definitions, poverty means material and social deprivation, the inability to participate in various societal activities. Canadian poverty researchers and international organizations such as the United Nations Development Program, United Nations Children's Fund, and Organization for Economic Co-operation and Development (OECD) agree that relative poverty – usually based on an individual or family income that is less than 50 per cent of the median national income – is the most useful measure for ascertaining poverty rates in wealthy developed nations such as Canada. These indicators show Canada performing very poorly in terms of poverty ranking: nineteenth of thirty industrialized nations for adults, twenty-first for families with children, and twentieth for children.[3]

Internationally, poverty is usually indicated if individual or family income is less than 50 per cent of the median national income. Statistics Canada's low-income measure (LIM) is the Canadian manifestation of this poverty measure. The more commonly applied low-income cut-off (LICO) identifies whether an individual or family is experiencing the "straitened circumstances" associated with spending significantly more than the average individual or family on basics such as food, housing, and clothing. The LICO can be calculated using either before-tax or after-tax income. Another commonly used measure is the market basket measure (MBM) devised by Human Resources Development Canada. All of these measures provide roughly comparable estimates of the incidence of poverty in Canada.[4]

Table 12.1
Poverty Rates for Various Groups, Canada and Ontario, 2007

	All Persons	Children	Unattached Females	Unattached Adult Males	Female-Led Families
			(as percentages)		
Canada	13.6	15.0	40.6	33.7	36.0
Ontario	12.9	14.5	42.5	35.5	36.4

Source: Statistics Canada, CANSIM System, Tables 202–0803 and 202–0805.

From an international perspective the Canadian figures for low-income, gathered by group and based on pre-tax LICOS, are very high (see Table 12.1). Especially striking are the very high figures for unattached adults, and this is especially the case for unattached female adults. Another aspect of the poverty situation in both Canada and Ontario is that the poor are not simply poor: they are very poor. The average gap between the LICO value and the average income of poor female-led families in Canada and Ontario is $9,600. The similar gap for poor unattached adult females (who represent two-fifths of all unattached attached females) is $9,100 in Canada and $9,300 in Ontario. For poor unattached adult males (about a third of all unattached adult males), the gap is $9,700 in Canada and $9,000 in Ontario. These figures indicate the presence of significant structural issues related to the distribution of income and wealth in Canada.

The existence of poverty in Canada is not difficult to understand. It reflects the means by which income is distributed in the society. Poverty levels are low when governments intervene in the unbridled operation of the market economy. Nations have lower poverty levels when they intervene by establishing more progressive taxation levels, transferring more national wealth to the population through universal benefits and programs, and making it easier for workers to operate under collective agreements supported by unionization of workplaces.[5] Nations such as Canada that let the marketplace determine the distribution of resources have high poverty rates.

Figure 12.1
Union Density, Collective Agreement Coverage, and Child Poverty, Early 2000s (coverage rates) and Mid-2000s (poverty rates)

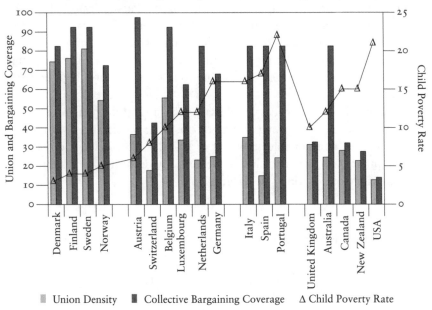

▦ Union Density   ▮ Collective Bargaining Coverage   Δ Child Poverty Rate

Source: Organization for Economic Co-operation and Development, "Trade Union Members and Union Density," 2006 http://www.oecd.org.

The factors of unionization rate, welfare benefits, and minimum wages can illustrate this point. Union density – or the percentage of workers belonging to a union – and collective agreement coverage are strongly related to the child poverty rate (see Figure 12.1). Social-democratic welfare states – Norway, Finland, Denmark, and Sweden – have the strongest unions and highest collective agreement rate and the lowest poverty rates. Liberal – or business-oriented welfare states – such as the United Kingdom, United States, Canada, New Zealand, and Australia have the opposite experience. The Continental European nations (conservative in politics, somewhat similar to Canada's Red Tories) have a union membership rate that is not as high as the rate in the social-democratic nations, but business and government do recognize the value of providing workers with various forms of security: their collective agreement rate is high, and their poverty rates are moderate. Italy, Spain, and Portugal are less wealthy and less developed welfare states whose poverty rates are similar to the liberal welfare states.

In Canada, belonging to a union brings higher wages and more benefits. This union advantage is especially great among less skilled workers –

who are also most likely to be poor. In Ontario the Liberal government refused to support a bill that would have reversed a law from the Mike Harris era and made it easier for workplaces to unionize. (In 2008 28 per cent of Ontario workers were unionized.) Passing this bill would have gone a long way to helping to reduce poverty.[6] This failure is consistent with market-based approaches that avoid intervention in the operation of the marketplace. While these approaches may keep the business sector happy, they do nothing to reduce Ontario's high poverty rate.

Individuals who receive social assistance in Ontario remain in a desperate situation. According to the OECD, social assistance is intended "not to give a reasonable standard of living."[7] To receive social assistance in Ontario, a person has to be virtually destitute, with almost no liquid assets of any kind (see Table 12.2).

Table 12.2
Welfare Assistance Situation for Persons in Ontario, 2008

	Single Person Considered Employable	Single Person with a Dis- ability	Lone Parent with Child Aged Two	Couple with Two Children Aged 10 and 15
Total Income	$7,352	$12,647	$16,683	$21,215
per cent at LICO	40	69	75	61
per cent at MBM	45	78	79	65
per cent Avg. Income	22	38	45	49
Liquid Assets at Application	$560	$5,000	$1,529	$2,017
Liquid Assets on Welfare	$560	$5,000	$1,529	$2,017
Benefits Decline from 1992	$4,048	$3,069	$5,761	$8,674
Percentage Decline	36	20	12	29

Source: National Council of Welfare, Welfare Incomes, nos. 1–4, Ottawa, 2010.

You not only must be virtually destitute to receive benefits, but also must remain that way to continue receiving them. In every case, benefits are well below various poverty lines. Crucially, some 50 per cent of applications for disability benefits are initially rejected, placing individuals into the frightening situation detailed for "single persons considered employable."[8] This reality – that individuals in Canada are forced to live in these circumstances – is shameful.

Finally, minimum wages in Ontario – now the highest in Canada – still place earners below the poverty line. The 2010 raise to $10.25 is a move in the right direction that needs to continue – because minimum-wage workers will still be earning about $1,500 per year below the poverty line.[9]

☐

Poverty is the primary determinant of children's intellectual, emotional, and social development. It is a strong predictor of virtually every adult disease known to medicine, including Type 2 diabetes, heart disease and stroke, arthritis, a variety of respiratory diseases, and some cancers. Childhood poverty increases the likelihood of poor health during adulthood. Given high child poverty rates, it should not be surprising that there has been an explosion of death from diabetes in low-income neighbourhoods in urban Canada.[10]

In addition to the statistical evidence on the effects of poverty, research has put a human face to the material and social deprivation experienced by impoverished Canadians.[11] Of particular value has been work documenting the social exclusion experienced by low-income Canadians and children's experience of poverty. Such narratives illustrate the clear links between material and social deprivation and immensely harmful outcomes.

Ontario's response has been to direct attention to the end of the sequence, setting up new and improved health, social service, justice, and police systems to deal with the effects of poverty. This work is carried out by those working in the health-care and public health systems; community agencies; and the education, social work, police and justice, housing, and nutrition sectors. Interventions can take place on many levels.[12] Further upstream come attempts to decrease the vulnerability of impoverished people by enhancing their coping skills: "We will not improve your living conditions, but we will attempt to provide you with the skills needed to cope with the deprivation associated with adverse living conditions."

These interventions do little to address the source of the afflictions: poverty. The emphasis is on making exposure to pitiful living conditions more palatable through the targeting of services. The extent to which these services can achieve success, considering the unfavourable living circumstances of impoverished people, is questionable. Interveners can also move even still further upstream and attempt to reduce the negative conditions to which impoverished people are exposed. Such interventions would include universal affordable child care, health and social services, and educational and recreational opportunities that are viewed as universal entitlements rather than as user-paid options. Many nations have moved to treat services and benefits not as commodities to be purchased on the market but as rights of citizenship. Their goal has been to reduce the detrimental effects of the social deprivation associated with poverty. Canada scores extremely low on these indices of decommodification.[13]

Perhaps the most efficacious means of reducing the effects of poverty would be to provide monetary resources to people so that they will not experience poverty in the first place. These resources would take the form of employment that pays a living wage, social assistance and disability benefits being raised to health-sustaining levels, and transfers to citizens on the basis of both universal entitlement and identified needs. In many European countries this is the approach that has proved the most successful.

The workings of our economic and political systems and the arguments that justify their approach have been nicely organized in research by Sébastien Saint-Arnaud and Paul Bernard, two Canadian sociologists who succinctly sum up the relationship between systemic differences in poverty rates and the development of different ways of addressing citizen security in terms of public policy.[14]

They indentify the United States, Canada, and United Kingdom as liberal welfare states, a formation that provides the least support and security to its citizens. In liberal welfare states the dominant ideological inspiration is individual liberty, and the dominant institution is the marketplace. The result is minimal government intervention in the workings of the marketplace. Indeed, such intervention is seen as providing a disincentive to work and as breeding "welfare dependence."

These nations provide minimal benefits to social assistance recipients, weak legislative support for the labour movement, meagre assistance for disabled people, and a reluctance to provide universal services and programs. The services and programs that do exist are residual, intended – but often failing – to provide the most vulnerable people with even basic needs. Of the developed nations, Canada ranks among the lowest in terms of public spending on infrastructure in general and on families, pensions, early childhood education and care, and supports for persons with disabilities. Canada's social assistance rates are among the lowest in the world. The results come in the form of extraordinarily high poverty rates.

The opposite situation prevails in social-democratic welfare states. Among the ideological inspirations for the central institution of these nations – the state – are equality, the reduction of poverty, and full employment. Government responsibility is not seen as limited to meeting the most basic needs of the most deprived. Rather, the organizing principle is universalism in terms of social rights. Denmark, Finland, Norway, and Sweden best exemplify this form of the welfare state. Governments with social-democratic political economies are proactive in identifying social problems and issues and in promoting the economic and social security of their citizens.

The social-democratic welfare state is associated with gender and class equality, the virtual elimination of poverty, and market regulation. Public policy is directed at supporting programs that serve to reduce social inequality – child care, services for those with disabilities, programs that address racism and homophobia, job training, and support for education.

Even welfare states that are considered conservative (France, Germany, the Netherlands) generally ensure a level of social security that is superior to the level provided by liberal welfare states. In conservative welfare states, the ideological favouring of social stability, wage stability, and social integration is expressed through the provision of benefits based on insurance schemes covering a variety of family and occupational categories.

☐

Poverty can be reduced by shifting the course of public policy-making. To improve the conditions experienced by Canadians living in poverty, public policy must be modified to ensure the provision of living wages, affordable food, housing, and quality child care. Achieving these goals will require pressure from both above and below.[15] Pressure from above will depend on elected leaders and policy-makers who will commit themselves to achieving these aims.

We see little evidence of this occurring in Ontario – which means that pressure from below by an aroused citizenry, together with those institutions concerned with health and well-being, will be crucial. A number of steps will help us to achieve these goals:

- educating the public that poverty is primarily a result of insensitive and uncaring public policy;

- showing that other jurisdictions have acted to reduce and in some cases almost eliminate the incidence of poverty;
- arousing the citizenry to demand similar public policy actions, and providing the means by which they can influence the behaviour of their elected representatives and policy-makers.

The document *Social Determinants of Health: The Canadian Facts* outlines how these objectives can be achieved.[16] It identifies numerous public policy options that would reduce poverty:

- increasing the minimum wage and boosting assistance levels for those unable to work;
- reducing inequalities in income and wealth through progressive taxation;
- making it easier for workplaces to unionize, because unionization serves to set limits on the extent of profit-making that comes at the expense of employees' health and well-being;
- creating a housing policy that provides affordable and quality housing;
- ensuring that provinces provide their matching share for housing provision as defined in the Affordable Housing Framework Agreement of 2001;
- increasing federal funding for social housing programs targeted for low-income Canadians.

The document also suggests courses of action that citizens can take to achieve these goals. These steps include: a) learning more about poverty and its causes; b) joining and/or supporting organizations that are working to reduce poverty; and c) contacting and calling for their elected representatives to take seriously the task of improving the living conditions that Canadians experience, with special emphasis on reducing poverty and improving health.

Poverty is a result of inequalities in economic and social resources brought about by imbalances in influence, wealth, and power. A key cause of poverty is that those with influence and power – and the elected representative and policy-makers who are the subject of their influence and power – see little need to reduce poverty. Only when these imbalances are addressed will we see serious efforts to reduce poverty and improve the health and well-being of Canadians.

13 Families Matter:
The Catch-22 of Poverty

> It is the children who pay for poverty. They get no food, no medicine. This is Canada, but we have poverty like a third world country.   – a mother from North Bay

ANGUISH AND FRUSTRATION: Lisa's voice told it all as she described the difficulty of being unable to pay for her daughter to participate in school pizza days or field trips. Stephanie, age nine, sat quietly at the Niagara audit as her mother talked about the family's constant struggle to get by.

Lisa tried to hide the pain in her voice as she explained how she often had to choose between putting food on the table and paying the bills. "Hopelessness and helplessness are big parts of my life."

Cynthia, a married mother of two, also attended the Niagara audit and told us about poverty's impact on her family life. Her husband had lost his job in November 2009, and the family eventually had to apply for social assistance. Cynthia sometimes sold baked goods to help pay the bills and make ends meet. She was making play-dough for her children because that was a kind of plaything the family could afford.

"We go without so our children do not have to. My little girl has tummy aches, probably stress-related. My little boy is such a good little boy. Sunday afternoon, he was raking leaves. He knows if he plants a seed, something will grow and we will have something good to eat, some good vegetables."

Despite the family's resourcefulness, they were finding it extremely difficult to make ends meet. The stress of living in poverty was hurting her relationship with her husband and, in turn, their relationship with their children. "My husband blows up because of his frustration."

Cynthia knew that her children had been suffering from the stress of living in poverty and the social stigma of lacking material possessions – how could they not? One day when Cynthia and the children were in the backyard, a neighbour yelled, "Why don't you go and get your welfare cheque and take the children to the park?" Cynthia acknowledged the hurtfulness of incidents like that.

"I try to teach my children control when it comes to food and to save some for tomorrow. We are getting used to accepting that this is the way life is. I try not to let my children cry. I wait until they go to bed and then I cry by myself in the bedroom."

Pauline, a married mother of two in Niagara Region, explained that even though her husband had a job, money was still tight because of the difficulties of surviving on one income. Every small measure to cut corners counted. She was buying her children's shoes several sizes too large because that way the footwear might last an extra season or two. She was not able to buy a new pair each year. Her children would not have had winter coats or snowsuits this past year if it had not been for the generosity of a local charity. Her son could not go to his friend's birthday party because Mother could not afford to buy a present for the party. It is difficult for her children to understand why their family has less than others.

"I have my kids watch shows on TV about starving children in Africa to help them learn to be more content with the little they have."

Jocelyn and Marc, in their early thirties, had three children between the ages of six and twelve. At the Niagara audit, Jocelyn described how aware her young children were of the family's financial state. One of her children received money as a gift for his birthday last year. He opted to buy the family milk instead of a present for himself. Jocelyn said it was heartbreaking when one of her children was invited to a social event with friends, such as a movie. She would have to say, "I don't have enough money to pay for the movie. You can't go."

Gail, a single mother of two in York Region, said she was trying to hide her financial troubles from her children in order to protect them.

"Last year when we got our Christmas hamper, my son was volunteering to help give out hampers to other people. On the way home he says, 'Mommy, I'm so glad we're not poor.' And I thought, 'I'm doing a good job at fooling you.'"

☐

Countless studies by psychologists, educators, and sociologists have demonstrated the negative effects of poverty on children and families. Poor children are less likely than are non-poor children to meet basic indicators of well-being that measure their physical health, cognitive ability, school achievement, and emotional or behavioural outcomes. Poor children are more likely than are non-poor children to have health issues, developmental delays, and learning disabilities. Poor children are also more likely to repeat a grade, drop out of school, be suspended or expelled, or have an emotional or behavioural problem that lasts for three months or longer. Child poverty is also, as one group of researchers points out, "associated with increased neonatal and post-neonatal mortality rates, greater risk of injuries resulting from accidents or physical abuse/neglect, higher risk for asthma, and lower developmental scores in a range of tests at multiple ages."[1]

The research reads like a battery of insurmountable obstacles.

The Family Stress Model developed by Dr. Rand Conger and his colleagues seeks to explain the processes through which poverty affects children. Conger, a distinguished researcher at the Institute for Social and Behavioral Research in Iowa, has conducted a series of studies over recent decades into the impacts of economic stress on children and families.[2] Research participants were of European-American or African-American descent. They lived in urban and rural settings and had a variety of economic backgrounds and family structures.

The research discovered what people who live on social assistance or a low income already know: economic hardship increases stress, which heightens family dysfunction. Parents are emotionally and mentally burnt out by their struggles to pay bills and provide for their children's basic needs, such as shelter and food. As parents become increasingly anxious and overwhelmed, spousal relationships are likely to suffer and disciplinary approaches may become inconsistent, creating further instability in the home. Ultimately, children bear the brunt of poverty.

A participant at the Toronto hearing captured this effect, saying: "Poverty is depressing. It affects the whole family."

Carla, from North Bay, described her personal experience with the processes described in the Family Stress Model: "Parents are stressed and they don't have the skills and resources to deal with the needs of their children. If a kid drops something, like food, his mother will slap him because there is not enough to begin with and they can't waste any. I was raised where you don't ask for a second helping and you don't tell anyone that there wasn't enough food."

A parent at the Ottawa audit commented, "I fell into depression last year. I had nothing to give my kids. It's not easy being a single parent."

Another woman living in North Bay commented: "Children suffer. There is abuse in the home, stress in the family resulting from poverty.

Children go to school hungry and can't learn properly. The body has to be fit to learn. It is not the fault of the parents."

The effects of poverty extend beyond a child's home life. The stigma of living in poverty is painful for children and youth, who find it difficult to understand why others have it so much easier. Constant bullying that centres around something like not being dressed in a certain way takes its toll. Parents who attended the audits described the social exclusion to which their children are subjected. The bullying, coupled with the extra costs of sending her children to school, led one mother in York Region to home-school her two teenage daughters.

"My children get teased because they don't have brand clothes. If you don't show up on day one in school with such clothes, then your kid is ostracized."

Not surprisingly, children learn quickly to hide their family's financial struggles from their friends and community members. One mother at the York Region audit recounted how her two teenagers kept the family's financial struggles a closely guarded secret from their peers.

"My kids were thirteen and fourteen during the time we were in a shelter, and to this day they still will not talk about it. They are embarrassed and mad at having to live there. Instead of telling their friends where they were, they say, 'Remember when we were at our aunt's?'"

Sharon, a single mother in Halton Region, knew all too well the multitude of ways in which poverty had an impact on her school-aged daughter, Laura. The young girl understood more about the family's financial state than she was letting on. She wanted things that other kids had, like iPods, but knew that her mother was struggling to provide the basics: food, hygiene products, school supplies. Laura told people that when she grew up, she wanted to make lots of money.

"Kids feel it more than parents realize. My daughter once said, 'Everyone else has it so much easier than us.' That hurts."

☐

Poverty and the stigma attached to it undermine children's social well-being in the schoolyard and their intellectual well-being in the classroom. The extra costs associated with school can be prohibitive for families on low incomes or receiving social assistance. Extra fees are often required to cover the cost of equipment and materials needed for high-school science and fine art classes. Children obviously enjoy being on school sports teams, joining clubs, and getting involved in other extracurricular activities – and the experiences are an important part of learning and growing. But these "extras" frequently come with added fees that prevent poor children from participating. For people living on limited incomes, a $40 school fee can be impossible to pay without significantly reducing funds for essentials such as food. At many of our social audits, parents expressed frustration and despair at their inability to pay such fees and about being unable to allow their children to participate fully in school.

At the Simcoe County audit, Natalia shared her wishes for her son, who has autism, to participate fully in school activities. Unfortunately, there is simply no room in her budget to pay for field trips. "My son once said, when he told me about a school trip to Quebec, 'It's okay Mommy, because I know you can't afford it.'"

Other parents reported that their children had stopped bringing home field trip forms because they knew their families could not afford to pay.

A handful of parents reported that their children's schools were able to help low-income families with these fees. At the Niagara Region audit, Alice said, "If there is a school trip and we don't have the money, the principal has told me they will help out." Another parent expressed gratitude to her extended family for assisting with the $40 fee for her daughter's high-school art class.

Shelley, a mother in York Region, expressed gratitude to a local charity for raising funds to subsidize the costs of program registration. "Operation Sparrow provides free recreation programs for children living in poverty. If it wasn't for Operation Sparrow, my kids wouldn't be doing anything."

Parents want their children to benefit from the social and educational value of arts and athletic programs, but the limited nature of social assistance is a clear barrier. Leanne, a recipient of ODSP and a mother of two teenagers in the York region, recognized the positive influence of sports on teenagers. Leanne had only $400 remaining after paying for rent each month, which left little room to pay for activities for her two children. She was fortunate in that she had her family to help out.

"My son is a high risk child, ADHD. He is a great athlete and is on the rugby team. There was a $120 uniform fee, plus shoes and everything else. My family is paying. If I can keep him in sports, it will keep him out of trouble. If not, he would be drinking, drugs, causing trouble if he wasn't in sports."

Other parents and children were not so lucky. "I can't afford to put my kids in sports activities," said Jake, a parent in North Bay.

"Registration, equipment, plus transportation to and from a game . . . it's too much."

Even basic school supply fees can exceed parents' budgets. School uniforms can be a huge expense for families living on low incomes. Binders, notebooks, and other supplies needed for school all add up. Parents at the Windsor audit expressed frustration with school policies requiring students to provide their own school supplies and, in some instances, both indoor and outdoor shoes.

"Many of us have no way of providing this. We either buy shoes or go hungry for the rest of the month."

In the information age, access to a computer and to the Internet has created a new divide between rich and poor. The "haves" gain access to a world of information and a new means of communication. The "have-nots" are left behind, excluded. Teachers expect students to have access to a computer, to hand in typewritten assignments, and to use the Internet at home to complete their school work. Although students in urban centres have access to computers at school or in public libraries, factors such as transportation costs or parents' work schedules will often prevent them from completing their homework assignments.

Dana, from the small village of Mountain, was working at three jobs to provide for her children. She had become acutely aware of how the family's lack of computer and Internet access had become not only a barrier to furthering her children's education but also a source of further stigmatization. "Children pay a price growing up in poverty. 'You don't have a computer? You don't have Internet?'"

Larissa had two teenage children and was living on employment insurance. She had been on a waiting list for subsidized housing for eight years. "I want to provide my kids with what they need and give them a normal teenage life – sit with their friends and have coffee, go to the movies, take them out for buffets once in a while. I don't have money for any of these things."

Jean, a single mother of three, had been on social assistance for thirteen years. She was unable to provide a computer and printer for her children at home, due to the family's tight budget.

"I have to argue with my children's teachers to tell them to stop sending them home with homework that needs to be done on the Internet. We can't afford Internet. We can't afford a printer so they can't type up their projects for extra marks. I'm still arguing with my son's gym teacher to stop sending him out in the rain. He only has one pair of shoes and if they get ruined, I can't afford another pair. If his shoes get wet, he has to wear them all day."

Another parent explained, "Education is affected by poverty. There's stress in the home. The child might drop out of school. The cycle of poverty is sustained. It's a vicious circle. It's hard to get out of."

□

Despite poverty's complexity and the myriad ways in which it damages the lives of children and their families, participants at all of ISARC's hearings raised two interrelated issues: you need a decent job to escape poverty, and, particularly for women, you need decent child care if you want to keep that job.

Affordable child care with flexible hours to meet parents' varied work schedules is hard to come by. Child care with strict hours limits the types of jobs that parents can look for. Child care that is further away may be inaccessible due to the added transportation costs. Even if an affordable child-care centre exists within a reasonable distance, it may have a waiting list one year long, or more. A lack of affordable and accessible child care also acts as a barrier to parents seeking education or training programs. A North Bay service provider who worked in early learning and parenting programming said, "It is hard to schedule a program like ours. Our young mothers with minimum-wage jobs have erratic schedules. They get short-notice call-ins for just a few hours of work. It is hard for them to commit to a weekly program."

Janet, a single mother who participated in the Peel audit, spoke of how a lack of affordable child care had prevented her from finding employment and getting out of poverty. She lost her job in 2007 and was forced to accumulate credit-card debt to provide at least temporarily for her children. She lived in a shelter for two months before finding an apartment she could afford. Janet had been on the waiting list for subsidized housing for seven years. In 2008 she completed the personal support worker program offered at colleges. Despite her new skill set, Janet had been unable to secure a job because child care is either unaffordable or incompatible with her children's schedules.

"I have two children, six and four. Both are in school and I'm on social assistance. It's hard. One starts school at 9 a.m. and the other at 1 p.m."

Another mother from Peel commented, "My child is too young to understand why Mommy cries. It's because of financial problems. . . . I can't break the cycle because I can't get affordable day care."

We also heard stories about women who stayed in abusive relationships because they could not afford child care.

Helen, a mother in North Bay, felt stuck because of the lack of affordable child care for her kids. She said that her struggle to find child care with extended hours, or even with before-school and after-school care, had severely damaged the quality of her and her children's lives.

"Shift workers can't get licensed day care at extended hours. It limits what kind of jobs we can look for. It also means that public transportation to early jobs or early college classes isn't possible because we can't get our kids to child care in the time that we need. My [social assistance] worker has an expectation that a friend can look after my kids, but I want good-quality day care where I know my child is safe and looked after well."

Brent, a former Ontario Works recipient who now worked for minimum wage in North Bay, understood this predicament all too well. "In order to get child care, you need to have a job. But in order to get a job, you need to have child care. It can be a real Catch-22."

Joseph Heller's famous novel, *Catch-22*, tells of a young U.S. air force bombardier who wanted to be grounded to avoid combat. The novel gave rise to the use of "Catch-22" as a term meaning a double bind, a situation in which one outcome is dependent on another and there is no escape from the dilemma. If a person wants to apply for social assistance, that person needs to have an address – but she or he can't afford to rent a place without first being on welfare. The person is caught in a Catch-22 situation.

Parents can easily find themselves caught in a similar state of affairs: unable to find work without child care, and unable to pay for costly child care without work. They are caught in a no-win situation, in a vicious circle with no clear means of escape.

14 Ontario's Push to Early Childhood Education and Care for All

Laurel Rothman

> We are faced with a situation that demands immediate action.
> – Royal Commission on the Status of Women, 1970

ONTARIO'S RECENT MOVE towards a full-day Early Learning Program (ELP) for all four- and five-year-olds is a landmark shift. It is something that provides a benefit not just for parents with young children, but also for prospective parents, early childhood educators, elementary teachers, child-care advocates, school boards, municipalities, unions, and low-income neighbourhoods. The commitment to establish a holistic learning and care program delivered by elementary teachers and early childhood educators working together in classrooms firmly establishes the primacy of universally accessible, publicly funded, and publicly delivered services for young children and their families.

This U-turn on the funding and delivery of services has the potential to move services from a patchwork situation, in which parents consider themselves lucky if they can find convenient, affordable high-quality child-care services, towards a system of neighbourhood-based integrated, affordable early learning programs in every community across the province. For parents, the ability to count on reliable services from January through December, in urban, rural, or suburban communities, whether they are in the paid labour force, in training or education or not, is highly valued. For Campaign 2000 and other advocacy groups, this move towards universality is long overdue.

As the Early Learning Program is implemented, we continue to monitor whether decision-makers are heeding the advice of an experienced municipal child-care leader who has contributed to the decades-long movement to achieve high-quality, affordable early childhood education and care services (ECEC) and who is well versed in the financial and service delivery aspects of ECEC services. This municipal leader advised the Legislative Committee reviewing the *Full-Day Early Learning Statute Law Amendment Act, 2010* to do three things to ensure the success of these dramatic changes:

- *do the right thing* – do make services universally accessible to all four- and five-year-olds;
- *do it right* – plan carefully with parents, service providers (school boards, municipalities, child-care programs), and other partners to ensure that they are informed and engaged; and
- *do it with the right resources* – put in place the physical, financial, and human resources necessary to ensure that the ELP provides the high-quality integrated service that Ontario parents want and need.[1]

Ontario's move to publicly funded, universally accessible ECEC services reflects the growing acceptance of the importance of the early years in human development for both children and society. While child development experts and many parents have recognized this key for years, the widespread understanding of the early years has only been acknowledged on the public agenda in recent years.[2]

Changes in the shape and size of the Canadian family are important factors that contribute to this broader appreciation of the value of the early years. In an aging society with increasing numbers of nuclear families, a shrinking child population, and high rates of mothers in the paid labour force (both lone mothers and those in couples), families want and need support in raising their children. The need and desire for publicly funded ECEC services are particularly acute and urgent for the more than 317,000 children (almost one in every nine children under eighteen) living in poverty in Ontario.

Child development research demonstrates that when ECEC programs are of high quality, they offer a strong foundation in cognitive, social, and emotional development that ideally complements the predominant influence of parents. The research convincingly shows that the positive effects of high-quality ECEC services often continue through elementary school. Furthermore, while all children gain from the experience of high-quality ECEC services whether or not their mothers are in the paid labour force, low-income children may benefit more. Thus, *doing the right thing* – that is, making services universally accessible to all four- and five-year-olds – logically flows from current research.

For all of these reasons, Ontario's shift towards affordable and available high-quality ECEC services is a bold initiative that has the potential to contribute to poverty reduction and social inclusion, support women's independence, and enrich child development for all children. What began as a 2007 Liberal Party election promise to introduce a full-day learning program for all four- and five-year-olds evolved into a centrepiece of Premier Dalton McGuinty's efforts to bolster education as a key strategy in making Ontario competitive. Dr. Charles Pascal, appointed as the Premier's early learning advisor, consulted widely in developing his comprehensive report, *With Our Best Future in Mind: Implementing Early Learning in Ontario*, released in 2009. The report reflected the growing consensus that child care and early education are inseparable, as Carol Bellamy, former executive director of UNICEF, observed.[3]

The report made numerous recommendations to create "a continuum of early learning, child care, and family supports for children from the prenatal period through to adolescence under the leadership of the Minister of Education."[4] The provision of a full-day Early Learning Program for all four- and five-year-olds – one that would free up child-care spaces for younger children and provide a high-quality program in publicly funded schools throughout a seamless day – is probably the item best known by the public. Significantly, parents would continue to choose how their children would participate, with the option of a half, full (school hours), or fee-based extended day of programming. For Campaign 2000 and other anti-poverty advocates, a key recommendation was the need to pay attention to low-income neighbourhoods as the program was phased in.

Starting in September 2010, the government began phasing in full-day learning for four- and five-year-olds. In the first year, nearly six hundred schools will offer full-day learning for up to thirty-five thousand students five days a week. Each following year the number of programs will be expanded, and the goal is to have the programs available in every school by 2015–16.

As families in Ontario in the twenty-first century struggle to balance work, family, and community life, the early learning programs will provide a valuable community asset that supports children's emotional, social, and education development while facilitating parents' ability to raise their children and to participate in community service, education, training, and paid employment. In a society in which more than 78 per cent of mothers with children of three to five years of age are in the paid labour force, and with almost one in every nine children under the age of eighteen living in poverty, this substantial commitment to a publicly funded, seamless early learning is timely and necessary.

The introduction of the Early Learning Program will have a significant impact on services that four- and five-year-old children now use and on services for children under four. With more than 90 per cent of four- and five-year-olds in Ontario now attending kindergarten at least on a part-time basis, it is reasonable to predict that most of them will be enrolled at least part-time in the new program. It is also expected that the four- and five-year-olds who now attend both kindergarten and licensed child care will enrol. Many of the families in the ELP will want extended day programs and will need child-care subsidies. Because of some short-sighted decisions, it is not likely that there will be sufficient additional funds to ensure that the new families using ELP who need subsidies for the extended day program will get them. Unfortunately, this is not an example of *"doing it with the right resources,"* as recommended.

As the government adopted legislation to implement the ELP, it is also most unfortunate that school boards were not obligated to provide integrated, extended-day programming during vacations and the summer break, as the Pascal report envisioned. Regrettably, very few school boards chose to provide the full-year program in the first phase of implementation. This failure left many young children with disruption and parents with the prospect of having to find other affordable, high-quality services for the summer. For many, this is not an incentive to enrol in the new ELP program. This aspect of change was not in sync with the recommendation to *"do it right."*

Another significant impact of the new ELPs is that community-based child-care programs will have fewer four- and five-year-olds. While one might argue that the child-care programs could then accommodate the critical need for services for more children of under four years, this is easier said than done. To follow the recommendation to *"do it with the right resources,"* considerable physical, financial, and human resources are needed to transform programs. In some communities this condition may be possible, but, as many of the community child-care programs report, a longer lead time for implementation is needed. As part of the implementation of the ELP, the province did announce a modest level of additional funding for subsidies (beginning at $6 million and growing to $51 million at full implementation) and light capital (up to $12 million in five years) for non-profit child-care centres. Still, these amounts are widely acknowledged as being far less than necessary.[5]

Where are we at in the struggle towards universally accessible, high-quality ECEC services? Ontario has made a major shift in policy direction that will benefit the majority of four- and five-year-old children and their families. For many young children, especially those in low-income families that could not previously get access to an extended day of learning and care because they could neither afford the service nor "win the lottery" for the scarce number of fee subsidies, full-day kindergarten will enrich their early years.

However, the Pascal vision of an integrated day for these children has become largely the introduction of full-day kindergarten, which may or may not be complemented by well-coordinated ECEC services within the school. The introduction of full-day kindergarten will widen the affordable early learning options for families but will not, as now structured and funded, achieve the optimum balance of high-quality ECEC services to support the needs of modern families throughout the calendar year.

It is fair to say that we are still struggling for universally accessible ECEC services to meet the needs of the twenty-first century.

15   "It's Not My Country Yet . . ."

IT IS COMMON FOR CANADIANS who are having trouble with their Internet service providers or their new digital cameras to remark jokingly that the person at the other end of the help line "sounded like they were in Mumbai." Those more knowledgeable about globalization and the rapid rise of the Indian software and computer help industries will invoke Bangalore, an important centre of India's computer-based industries.

Yet things are not always as they seem.

"I got a job here in Canada at a call centre," explained Prabha at the Brantford social audit. "I am a lawyer in India and practised for eight years. I gave up my files to come to Canada and was married for three months. The abuse started and I had no money. I lost my self-esteem, my confidence. I lost the person I used to be."

The voice at the end of the line may sound South Asian. But the person telling customers how to reset to factory default settings may well be in a Southern Ontario city named for Mohawk leader Joseph Brant (Thayendanegea), who helped newcomers 250 years ago. Those arriving in Brantford in the early twenty-first century must cope with challenges no less formidable than wilderness and the rigours of North American winters.

"I came here from Vietnam fifteen years ago," said Mai. "I have been on Ontario Works for ten years. I have three children. The first child died at birth. My husband is also from Vietnam. The marriage broke down, and I left him and had to stop work because the pressure was too high."

Single women, particularly single mothers, face daunting obstacles in escaping poverty. This is true of women whose families have been in

Canada for generations, but the problems are magnified for women who have arrived more recently and whose cultures are not welcoming to non-traditional families and the realities of single parenthood. All the women in the Brantford group session nodded in agreement when they heard these words:

"We are 'bad' because we are not with our husbands. This is not a good thing in our culture. I am alone."

"I went to the shelter," said another woman. "It was equal to being killed because it was not acceptable to my ethics. I was told by Ontario Works workers that it was my choice to come to Canada. I was asked 'Why did you come to Canada?' They made the presumption that I married to immigrate and that I was using the system."

Aside from the stigma of separation, participants also agreed that dealing with the authorities was another source of stress.

"The letters I received from Legal Aid and Ontario Works are threatening," said one. "I don't understand the documents. I panic because of the tone and the language."

"When I was in subsidized housing I paid rent on time every month," said another. "I was two days late and the cheque cleared my bank account. I received an eviction notice. I called and they told me not to worry about it. Not to worry about it! It's a legal document. Do they think immigrants are stupid idiots and do not know anything? This happens a lot. These letters are common."

These accounts, from a single social audit, represent only a glimpse of the myriad sets of problems faced by immigrants struggling to make a life for themselves in their newly adopted homeland. These problems include learning a new language, finding work, and getting credentials accepted. Then there is the reality of racism – individual and systemic discrimination. The situation faced by immigrants of colour (also known as visible minorities) amounts to social exclusion. Toronto academic researcher Grace-Edward Galabuzi has described social exclusion as the inability of individuals or groups to participate equally and fully in the life of a society. Such exclusion is most often the result of inequality with respect to money, connections, and political power. It is linked to issues of class, race, gender, and disability.[1]

It is commonplace to describe Canada as a nation of immigrants, the first group being Northern Europeans who pushed aside the original peoples, whose subsequent experience remains a definitive case study in social exclusion. Canada has also been resource-rich but people-poor, and has always been forced to import labour to meet its needs. Chinese workers built the first cross-country railway, Ukrainians populated the

Prairies, Southern Europeans built the postwar cities. But in Ontario today things have shifted away from the historical pattern. Within seven years over half of Toronto's population will be people of colour. Non-European families make up 37 per cent of all Toronto families, but account for 59 per cent of poor families.[2]

People who have recently arrived in Ontario (overwhelmingly from Asia) are confronted with a labour market that has shifted dramatically since previous waves of immigration. With the rise of precarious employment – part-time, temporary, contract work – people of colour increasingly find themselves stuck in dead-end survival jobs even though many well-qualified people arrive with high expectations about their new homeland. As the Windsor social audit heard again and again, government policies "make it nearly impossible to move ahead."

In Waterloo we heard about the massive barrier faced by newcomers who could not get their credentials recognized. This underlined stories that have become tragically commonplace: physicists driving taxi; physicians pushing brooms; people with sophisticated skills and high expectations suddenly discovering that their credentials do not count in Canada. This pattern forces newcomers to go back to school, which is a costly undertaking during a time when money and jobs are scarce.

Participants at Waterloo's Sunnydale Community Centre included a woman who had come to Canada nineteen years earlier. Her blind husband and her children were relying on the Ontario Disability Support Program and had come to see that a telephone, a car, and even shoes were necessities in Canada, not luxuries. But now her teenage children were asking for brand-name shoes and clothes and felt stigmatized by wearing used clothing. She realized the importance of social networks that are the staple recommendations at any job-finding course.

"I have found the paths," she said. "I go and meet lots of people who can help me by visiting and helping at community centres. But many people do not know how to do this."

She struggled with transportation and lived in fear of higher gas prices or a sudden breakdown. And although she was grateful for the drug benefits, she had also experienced the feeling of being at the end of a leash being pulled by an anonymous bureaucracy. For example, when her daughter graduated from high school the young woman immediately got a job to help out with the family finances. The social assistance authorities got wind of this and demanded benefit repayments, forcing the daughter to move out of the family home. Yet the calls still kept coming.

"Where is she?"

"She moved out. Check your files."

This proved highly stressful, as were the regular requests from the children still at home. They would ask her for money and when she said she had none, she often heard, "Why don't you go to the bank?"

Another Waterloo mother arrived in Canada in 2005. Back in Pakistan, her family was reasonably well off, and it had never occurred to her to think about the cost of food. Now, with three children, Farah had to budget relentlessly. She also planned ahead for the day when her employment insurance would run out, forcing her onto Ontario Works. After paying for basic expenses, she had $280 left for food.

Farah was grateful for the help she had received from social assistance. As a politically conservative person, she believed that the government should put limits on the amount of time that an able-bodied person can collect benefits. She wanted her children to understand the importance of struggling and not depending on the government.

"I don't want you to work in a warehouse," she told her oldest son, who graduated with a 93 per cent average and was now pursuing an engineering degree.

Yet she found herself getting anxious when her kids saw what their schoolmates had, and she knew she could not provide the same things. Then the inevitable questions would come up. "Why can't they have these things?" "Why don't we have money?" "Why can't you get a job?" One son would often come home and ask, "Mom, did you get a job or not?"

☐

The stories of immigrant doctors driving taxis have come to symbolize the treatment of recent arrivals. Canada's needs are neglected along with the welfare of newcomers. Yet historical patterns of the exploitation of working-class immigrants persist. In 2010 the Chinese Interagency Network of Greater Toronto surveyed newcomers and found that two of three had no knowledge of overtime rules. Some 40 per cent did not know they were protected by basic labour laws or that there is a minimum wage. Chen arrived from China in 2006 and found herself getting $25 a day for a seven-day week. The workday lasted ten hours. "You just accept what you are given."

There is a fear factor here. Like generations of other immigrants, vulnerable and poorly educated newcomers face intimidating employers and language and literacy challenges. Ill-informed and fearful, they are reluctant to make waves. Beixi Liu of the Toronto's Workers' Action

Centre explained that changes in labour laws proposed by Bill 68 would force workers with complaints to first confront their employers before going to the Ministry of Labour. Liu described this as unreasonable and intimidating for workers already scared of their bosses.[3]

While nearly three out of every four immigrants to Ontario has a university education, visible minority people still make up 40 per cent of workers in the sewing and fabric industries, and 36 per cent of taxi drivers. Only 3 per cent of executives are from racialized groups. Temporary help workers, disproportionately people of colour, earn 40 per cent less than permanent workers doing the same jobs. And although recent immigrants have more education than those who arrived in the past, chances are they will remain poor. Indeed, between 1981 and 2001 the number of immigrants, mainly people of colour, who are poor in Toronto rose by 125 per cent.[4]

One social audit took place at Toronto's Mennonite New Life Centre, an agency that serves newcomers and provides help with settlement, language courses, and translation services. With three branches in Toronto, the Centre is an important place to which immigrants turn. Mariana arrived in 2004 from Colombia. Describing the issues confronting newcomers, she mentioned first of all, not surprisingly, the difficulty that internationally trained professionals have in finding work in their fields. Their standard of living plummets and frustration mounts. The New Life Centre has added programs in anger management.

"What does it mean to succeed?" Mariana asked, before describing the Catch-22 so familiar to new Canadians. "Not just to get a survival job, but meaningful work that uses your skills and talents. The problem is getting 'Canadian experience.' If you don't have it, it's hard to get it. It's a vicious circle."

She participated in a study that found that over half of newcomers had annual incomes of less than $20,000 annually. People try to find work, but they are also busy studying English.

Juan, also from Colombia, agreed. He reported that Canada's professional societies had closed their ranks against immigrants. "They want to protect their own fields, keep the jobs for themselves and the newest crop of Canadian-trained professionals."

Juan's own legal experience gave him particular insights into the dynamics of discrimination. He believed that much resistance to newcomers probably springs from cultural factors. But the breakthroughs that can be achieved will also be rooted in culture.

"Those who have faced barriers themselves are more likely to help because they know the feeling," he added. "For instance, I was given a chance by a lawyer who was a Black man. He too had experienced barriers when he was starting out and was willing to give me a chance."

But Juan had also noticed that this condition can cut both ways: "In Canada you will find certain sectors dominated by former immigrant groups. These people will tend to protect their own communities, so they will tend to either shut out or pay less to workers from other ethnic backgrounds."

One entry point, often emphasized in job-finding clubs, is internships. Getting a job as an intern – or simply volunteering – can provide a foot in the door, and it can provide useful experience. Juan understood the strategy, yet he emphasized the temporary nature of such free labour and remarked that reference letters that do not spring from a formal, employer-employee relationship can be hard to get. Moreover, he explained, "It's not really an option for a newcomer not to have an income."

Mariana had thought a lot about the pressures and stresses under which immigrant families struggle. Her insights reflected the experience of Farah in Waterloo. Mariana noticed that many qualified professionals "end up taking 'survival jobs.' . . . They give up their own expectations and focus on the next generation."

She noted that the average income among newcomers had not increased in the six years since she arrived in Canada.

"We need to deal with poverty among recent immigrants and its effect on children. Parents who need to take several low-paying jobs just to make ends meet are rarely home, and the children are attracted to gangs."

Many women arrive in Ontario's bigger cities not to look after their own children but to care for those of Canadians who can afford live-in child-care labour. But this is often another dead end, Mariana explained. "If you arrive in Canada on a child-care visa, you have no right to apply for permanent residency. You have no rights. Really! This is something that affects a lot of Filipina woman."

Still, both Juan and Mariana remained hopeful about programs like Newcomers' Skills at Work: Refusing to Settle for Less, through which Latin American and Chinese immigrants are becoming empowered by learning to understand the system and becoming agents of change. They believe these kinds of programs will make a difference.

"We're not asking for special treatment," Mariana insisted. "Just for open doors."

Ontario has, of course, always opened its door to newcomers. Immigration has driven the province's growth – from the time that Joseph

Brant joined the Loyalists to the British crown who fled the American Revolution, and the days of the Germans who colonized parts of rural Southwestern Ontario and the Finns who logged and mined in Northern Ontario, to the Italians and Portuguese who laid the bricks in Toronto's suburbs.

In one respect, little has changed. Ontario will in the future depend heavily on immigrants for its prosperity. But in another respect, the changing face of newcomers means that the province will be relying on people of colour to meet its looming skill shortages. In a 2004 study the Conference Board of Canada pointed out that this group is *already* contributing a disproportionately high proportion of real gross domestic product (GSP). In the period the Board measured (1992–2001), visible minorities accounted for 0.3 per cent per year of the growth in the real gross domestic product. That was when they accounted for 11 per cent of the labour force. By contrast, the remaining 89 per cent of workers contributed only 0.6 per cent of real GDP growth.

"Relative to the rest of the population, then, the contribution of visible minorities is disproportionately large," the Board concluded. It added that inequality was dragging everyone down. "As strong as the contribution of visible minorities is, it could be even stronger were it not for the 14.5 per cent wage gap that exists. And this gap is a persistent one, and it's even deepening. Data show that the wage gap has widened over the last decade, going from 11 per cent in 1991 to the current 14.5 per cent."[5]

While these are Canadian figures, they surely reflect the situation in Ontario, the province that attracts more immigrants than any other. By 2016 one in five workers will be from a visible minority group. With eight of every ten Canadian immigrants being visible minorities, we cannot afford to allow them to languish in poverty, their skills ignored.

□

The Peel Region social audit heard from several newcomers whose experience exposes the thorny thickets that they fall into in their new homeland. One refugee, a licensed massage therapist, had hoped that his trade, coupled with his formal information technology qualifications, would stand him in good stead. He found, however, that his only option was to obtain Canadian equivalency because his skills, training, and talent were not formally recognized here. He was taking English classes and hoping for the best. Asked if there was one thing he could change, he quickly answered, "It's not my country yet. I just want to pay Canada back for what it has done in my life."

One of the things he said he had learned was to navigate the system that would, he hoped, provide him with the means to live. He described his confusion about talking to a machine on the telephone as an interactive voice response system told him what to do next. Then, each time he did manage to get through to a real person, he had to keep repeating his story again and again. The process was repeated when he had to physically manoeuvre himself through the system. The distance between social assistance offices and his utter lack of knowledge of what was happening to him compounded his confusion.

He recalled having to travel north from Mississauga to the Peel Region office in Brampton after being told that the paperwork he needed could not be completed in Mississauga. After finally arriving at the Brampton office he learned that before anything else could be done he first had to register through the Internet. Why, he asked himself, had he not been told that in Mississauga? Yet despite his trials he remained grateful for the opportunity to enter the Canadian mainstream with a decent-paying job.

A woman who spoke to the York Region social audit reflected the remarkable gratitude that newcomers feel when they get a chance to make a new start in Canada. "In the last two years my income was reduced 90 per cent. I am on welfare and I am thankful to Canada for that, but it is very difficult. I receive $1,000 to cover rent, food, etc. I would like to provide for my family as well. I have family abroad. I told them Canada is a great country. In case they come here I want to take care of them."

Despite all the positive feelings, the experiences of the newcomers mirrored those of the hundreds of other low-income people who attended the social audits.

One immigrant mother who spoke to us was living in subsidized housing in Mississauga with her five children. She said she was constantly worried about both the drug activity in her neighbourhood and the heavy police presence. She was genuinely fearing for her children. Compounding the situation, one of her children had been diagnosed with schizophrenia. Her husband did not live with the family because of illness and addiction issues, and he was also a constant concern. The authorities had reduced her income because they thought she was lying about her husband not living with the family. She insisted to them that he had moved out because he knew his problems were harming all of them. She received assistance from ODSP, but was in need of medication and particular foods to deal with her diabetes. Her dietary needs remained unmet because she had to get by on what she could afford.

She broke into tears when she began to wonder aloud to the rapporteurs about what she could possibly do for her son. She even blamed
herself for his condition, and her guilty feelings were compounded by
comments she was receiving from her family back home. Her relatives
blamed her for deciding to come to Canada and for the woes that followed. She was torn over whether to return to her home country. She
said that it was her spiritual faith that kept her going.

Another woman in Peel Region arrived in the Greater Toronto Area
and immediately got help from a shelter where she initially stayed with
her four children. The shelter staff found her a place to live, but her
social assistance cheque left little for food, so she was depending on the
food bank. A single mother, she had been able to get a few contract jobs
that had not generated enough cash to get her children into programs
that would get them used to life in a new country and, most importantly to her, keep them physically active. Getting around the sprawling
suburbs was a huge challenge. Although she was once receiving help
with bus tickets, budget cuts had eliminated this assistance. She, too,
said that her spiritual faith kept her going.

The social audit also heard from a refugee who arrived in suburban
Toronto in 2008. He had been working on short-term contracts to supplement social assistance and food bank support for his family of four.
When he spoke to us he was excited because he had just landed a job
interview with a major courier firm. Although he remained optimistic, he
said that if he could change anything it would be the attitudes of the
social assistance staff – he thought they should better understand the
power they were wielding. Although they were available when he needed
to consult them, they were ready to cut him off if he was not carrying the
right piece of paper. "They need to be slower on the trigger."

A Colombian woman told us about fleeing violence in her homeland, where her husband had been a bank manager and she had taught
Spanish and French. The family of four received Ontario Works assistance on arrival. They rented two bedrooms in another family's house
for $750 a month before moving to an $850 two-bedroom basement
unit. Before latching onto the three jobs she was now holding, this
mother had to get food bank assistance. She said she was determined to
have her teaching qualifications recognized in Ontario even though the
Ontario College of Teachers process would cost her $1,500 that she did
not have. Her eighteen-year-old daughter wanted to quit school to get a
job, but the mother would not allow it.

☐

There is an old superstition, said to be common among people hoping to make a new life in North America. The story had it that the streets "were paved with gold." Perhaps people half believed this, perhaps not. But like many a myth, its importance lies in the telling of the story. And, this tale continued, when the migrants arrived here they quickly learned three things: the streets were not paved with gold; indeed, they were sometimes either not paved at all or badly in need of repaving; and it was the newcomers who were expected to pave them. The story says enough about the immigrant experience that Italian-born Toronto photographer Vincenzo Pietropaolo, whose father did indeed work in construction, titled one of his books *Not Paved with Gold: Italian-Canadian Immigrants in the 1970s.*[6]

The social audit showed us that some things have not changed since Vincenzo came to Toronto in the 1950s. We found out that immigrants to Ontario remain hopeful and determined, grateful for the chance to fashion a new life for themselves and eager to contribute, as so many have in the past, to their adopted country.

But we also learned from the recent immigrants who were kind enough to share their experiences with us that much has changed since the 1950s when Southern Europeans had to struggle against perilous conditions and discrimination in the building trades and sweatshops. Jobs in construction and factories, jobs that once paid a living wage in good measure due to the organizing efforts of immigrants themselves, are no longer plentiful. People arriving from Pakistan, Somalia, or Colombia are now confronted with a split-level job market, and they become consigned to the basement of that market, where they must scramble to obtain even the most precarious part-time or temporary work. What is more, most of the newcomers are from Asia. The Conference Board of Canada described the growth of our visible minority population as "staggering."

Visible minority migrants are earning far below their potential because of the systematic discrimination that has plagued newcomers to Canada since Chinese men arrived to build the Canadian Pacific Railway. Coupled with a changing job market and government's hands-off policies in dealing with shady employers (see chapter 4), what this means is that even as the population of visible minority migrants skyrockets as a percentage of the population, their potential is wasted. Their eagerness to contribute is frittered away. It is against this background that social justice advocates launched a Colour of Poverty campaign and an academic researcher called his book on the social exclusion of racialized groups *Canada's Economic Apartheid.*

"I was on Ontario Works for a few months," one newcomer reported to the Brantford social audit. Then she added, in a way that reflects the expectations of so many, that her situation had improved. "I am now working but not in my profession. I am not earning much money."

16 Rural Poverty: Hidden in the Country?

The poor stay poor, the rich get rich
That's how it goes
Everybody knows.
— Leonard Cohen

THE HOUSE OF LAZARUS SITS on County Road 1 on the outskirts of the rural hamlet of Mountain in Southeastern Ontario. The brick structure is surrounded on three sides by corn and hay fields and pastures where cattle graze. The bucolic setting is not exactly the kind of place where you would expect to find a food bank. Yet the sprawling establishment – it includes thrift and household goods shops as well as a warehouse – is like many similar help centres started in the 1980s. It hosts a Coins for Kids Lunch Program to help families who often cannot afford school lunches, and, all in all, this ecumenical outreach mission serves some six hundred people from Kemptville and Prescott to Spencerville and Iroquois.

"It feels like chaos on caffeine most days," said Executive Director Pauline Pratt. "And yet there's a serenity in the goings-on that I attribute to the volunteers and staff that run the operations. Many say it feels like home."

Poverty in rural Ontario is the same as it is in the big cities. Children going without school lunches. People struggling to start over after an unlucky shift in their circumstances. Yet, as ISARC's social audit discovered in our first probe of poverty among our country neighbours, it can look a lot different. Difficulties with transportation and problems such as isolation and stigma take on a different form in the countryside.

Living in poverty is an isolating experience wherever you live, but in rural areas the lengthier distances between one place and another compound the isolation. What's more, the low-income cut-off (LICO) levels are lower for rural areas than for urban areas. And since the LICO is a frequently used measure of poverty, this determinant suggests that people in poverty in rural areas are not "as poor" as people in urban centres are. A popular misconception has it that food security is not an issue in rural areas because people can produce their own food. Housing is also seen as being substantially cheaper and easier to find.

Statistics Canada defines "rural" as any population centre with fewer than ten thousand people. The rural social audits ranged from conversations with people living on the fringes of larger centres to those living away from even the smallest population centre. Rural does not automatically mean agricultural. While most rural people in Southern Ontario do not live far from farmland, not everyone is a farmer. Nor does everyone have access to land. Rural may also mean living in the small logging or mining settlements that dot Northern Ontario's boreal forest belt.

Travelling to seek help at a place like the House of Lazarus can be hard. And the experience is often no less difficult when you get there, and that is because "people talk."

"People talk when we go into the food bank," explained Alicia, a single mother in Kent County. "Everybody knows."

☐

"I ride into school with a friend, but that means I am there hours before my class," a single father told the Wilmot social audit. "After class I can take a bus home, but living so far from the city means that the bus ride is hours long. I'm hoping that at the end of this schooling I will be able to find a job, though I don't know how I will be able to get to work if I live where I do now."

The biggest single obstacle facing rural people living on poverty-level incomes is transportation. Public transit is either non-existent or sporadic. Taxis, an expensive option at the best of times, are rare in some areas. If you live beyond walking distance of services, how do you get there? Friends are not always available to offer a ride when you need it, so owning and maintaining a car can be your only choice. But cars cost money to buy, insure, maintain, and fuel. What do you do when you are confronted with the choice between putting gas in the car or food on the table?

"I don't have a car and have to walk everywhere, using a cart to bring things home," said Wendy, a woman who attended the Kent County social audit. "I'm getting older and in winter cannot get all the groceries I need."

Those who took the time to attend each of our rural audits identified transportation as a major issue. Government and health-care providers – to say nothing of affordable shops – have centralized services. Some people told us that they do not use food banks because they simply cannot get to them. Others described the lengths they went to keep their car, their lifeline, on the road. A Kent County rapporteur summed up the problem.

"You need a vehicle when you live in rural areas. To get to work, to centres where shopping, banking, medical care, social services, food banks are located. This may mean travelling to several different towns."

Transportation problems compound feelings of isolation. The harder it is to make it into town to shop, keep appointments, or just meet other people, the more likely it is that people will become socially isolated. There is a real risk that they will drop right out of community life. This adds a new face to the notion that rural communities are tightly knit places with a rich community life. While this can certainly be true, poverty has an effect on the quality of life far beyond its economic weight. The ability to move from one place to another is essential for everything from working to meeting with friends and family. Keeping in touch with others is the stuff of life.

So too is keeping an affordable roof over our heads. Housing is just as big an issue in the country as it is in the city. There simply is not enough social housing stock available, and waiting lists are long. Single people and large families in particular have an even greater difficulty finding suitable places to live because not much housing is available for people at the extremes of family size. A Huron County single mother said that she and her four children had long lived in what was essentially a two-bedroom house.

"We were constantly pressured by CAS [Children's Aid Society] to get a bigger house, but I couldn't afford it," this mother said. "My four children worried constantly about being forced to leave. If they [CAS and the social housing provider] would have listened and noticed that a bigger house was needed, it would have been a big difference for us. It took years to find a place big enough that I could afford."

When she met with our rapporteurs in Huron County, another single mother raised an issue that recurred in discussions across the province – the way that housing and social assistance policies tend to promote family breakup when teenagers reach the age of eighteen. "I'm in housing now, a nice apartment, but my daughter is living on the streets. I wanted her to live with me but housing wouldn't allow it. I had to ask her to leave."

In 2008 Canada's Senate Committee on Agriculture and Forestry published the results of its cross-country research study *Beyond Free Fall: Halting Rural Poverty*. As with ISARC's findings about poverty in rural and small-town Ontario, it explained that appearances can be deceiving. "On the surface, there is no rural housing problem. The rate of home ownership in rural Canada is considerably higher than in urban Canada; and as the committee emphasized in its interim report, it is rare to see a homeless person in rural and small town Canada. Nevertheless, the committee found that there are serious housing problems, namely poorly-maintained homes and significant pockets of 'hidden homelessness' across rural Canada but especially in the nation's more remote northern regions."[1]

Some low-income people choose not to live in social housing because they believe that the housing or the neighbourhood is not safe. As one Huron County woman said, "I want to choose where I live."

Yet paying market rent can mean spending as much as 80 per cent of your income on housing – and market rent does not necessarily mean high-quality shelter or even comfortable accommodation. Many people rent old farmhouses only to end up paying more for heating than they do on rent. Some live in buildings that were never meant to be houses. Others end up with no fixed address. Those who make it to the top of the affordable housing waiting list, said Alicia, face challenges. "The only inspection they do in social housing is to see how much the tenant maintains the apartment, not what the landlord needs to maintain. Steps are broken in my backyard, and this is a danger to my children."

A service provider told the Huron social audit that, in rural areas, "It is very hard to recognize that people are homeless. We call it couch-surfing – like there is no box on the side of the road, but there is a friend's couch, or people are living under bridges in tents. People are living in places not meant to be housing."

The rural homelessness problem looks very different than it does in the city. It may still mean couch-surfing, but it can also mean living in a tent or a vehicle in someone's bush. As in cities, many homeless people are very young. Though there are very few shelters, these emergency places are starting to appear. Another challenge is that many homeless youth lack identification. Without ID, you cannot obtain social assistance, you can't apply for social housing, and sometimes you can't even get help from food banks. Not all of the homeless head for cities. Some youth in the country have little idea as to where they will be sleeping on any given night.

"I lived in a church-run housing project when I was released from the military. My living quarters were cramped and there was lots of drug abuse, drunkenness, theft, and violence," said a man in Kent County. "When I applied for jobs, I couldn't give my phone number for fear another tenant would answer."

The county warden in Huron suggested building new housing units on land already owned by the county. The spaces would be primarily for seniors, with rents starting at $428, almost 80 per cent of the $580 provided monthly by Ontario Works. But he also expressed frustration about trying to make programs designed for cities work in the country. "If local government could make the decisions on how to spend provincial funds, they could make local solutions for local problems."

□

A 1965 Canadian government study heard from poor families: "As long as we live in the country we will never starve."[2] Yet today half of the food banks in the nation are in rural areas, and sixty rural food banks have opened since 2000.[3] Soup kitchens are also making an appearance. Gardens are a good solution to the need for cheap and healthy food, but they require land, seeds, and other inputs – besides only providing food for a limited number of months in the year. Even gathering berries requires transportation to get to the berry patch.

"I can't afford healthy food, so some days I just don't eat," a single mother in Niagara said. Her words reflected a depressingly common theme underlined by so many others across Ontario.

The country is not, then, a place in which the "poor will never starve." Rural people living in poverty need to get to town to buy food or visit the food bank. Many food banks limit their clients to weekly or even monthly visits. In Niagara Region the mother of a family of five, including a teenager, a ten-year-old, and a six-year-old, described their dilemma: "We are a one-income family making far below $20,000, and when we run out of money, we have to choose between paying the hydro or paying the rent, buying cough syrup for a sick child or buying milk. Life is a constant struggle."

Health and poverty are closely related. Transportation to medical appointments and other services remains a major issue for people living in poverty in the rural areas. An elderly woman in Huron described her chronic shortness of breath and her struggles to get by. "I use Meals on Wheels, but I still need to pay for that while being on a budget of less than forty dollars a month. I also need to buy vitamins because of my illness, but I can't afford them."

Underlining another common theme across the province, a disabled

man in Mountain discussed the stress of a low-income life that is compounded by extra costs that might seem minor to many. "I am constantly
frustrated and depressed. I need to go to Ottawa for doctor's appointments, but for ODSP to cover transportation costs I need the doctor to
complete a form for proof of travel and there is a $50 fee for that."

Transportation challenges have been intensified by the provincial
government's cost-cutting measures that centralize services away from
small communities. It is becoming ever more difficult for people to
make it to distant hospitals and clinics. A social audit convenor
summed it up: "There is a shortage of doctors in many rural communities and many small hospitals are in jeopardy of closing. Even pharma-
cists are disappearing from rural communities."

Food and shelter insecurity compromise health, wherever you live.
Hungry children are less likely to perform well at school. If they fall far
enough behind, playing catch-up becomes impossible. Broadband connections are more expensive in rural areas, and Internet access has
become necessary for homework. The problem of having access to the
required technology is just another price paid by children growing up in
poverty. "*You don't have a computer??*" "*You don't have Internet??*"
For a family in Mountain, stigma and exclusion are added onto the educational cost of not being able to afford to do homework.

Poverty grinds away at children not simply by depriving them of a
decent diet. Children whose parents cannot afford to pay fees for school
activities such as sports and field trips become isolated from their peers.
Some programs provide special allowances, but small-town life makes
the charity cases stand out. The stigma of the brand bullies adds to the
exclusion when youth just can't seem to fit in.

"Kids are labelled because mom is on welfare, because they don't
wear designer shoes," a single mother told the Huron social audit.

Family life can be – and as our provincial audit reveals, often is –
shattered by poverty. Low-income parents of teenagers turning eighteen
face an agonizing situation. When a child turns eighteen, the family
loses crucial family child tax credits. The loss in turn creates an expectation on the part of government service providers that the existence of
another "adult" household member means that the family now has
another income. In these circumstances parents can no longer afford to
let their children live at home. They are forced to decide whether they
have to ask their children to leave.

"They cut my cheque when my son turned eighteen," a single
mother told the Huron audit. "My family has already been torn apart
[by divorce], and now it will be again."

Another single mother was quick to agree. "I have the same situation with my daughter. It's either she stays with me and I get deducted or she moves out. But I can't help my daughter move out."

All of which prompted a teenager acting as a recorder at the audit to reflect on what she had just learned: "What I'll never forget about this experience is how lucky I am." For her, "the stories local women shared with us about their teenage sons and daughters potentially being forced to move out so that they can make ends meet" were "a sickening idea."

Children from low-income families frequently face the issue of housing instability. An eviction notice or even just the necessity of moving to seek a better job or get access to services brings disruption and stress. In rural areas, a move from town to the country means a new school, a new peer group. A Huron County single mother asked, "Do I uproot her [daughter who has just settled at school, made friends] because my personal life is slacking to move to another community where there may be better services or opportunities?"

Because the experience is so intimately linked to social class and the bad luck of being born to low-income parents, young people finding themselves outside of the family home (due to arcane and cruel social assistance rules of family breakdown) often face a daunting situation. They may have lacked opportunity as young children and have lower educational outcomes. If they end up on the street, they will also face the cost of acquiring legitimate personal identification. According to a Huron County service provider, "We have a lot of kids who have no identity, no birth certificate, no licence. If they don't have a piece of ID they can't get a piece of ID. It costs money to get that ID. With no ID they can't get anything: no library card, no Ontario Works. If there are problems in the home, kids can't get these documents from their parents."

☐

"Poverty is not changing," a Kent County social services worker said. "People are stuck. Most distressing is that the stigma of poverty has never changed."

A strong sense of independence and self-reliance is not new for people living in rural communities. Yet for rural people living in poverty, feelings of humiliation and shame permeated many of the stories that we heard during the social audit.

"I have lost my dignity," a Huron County woman said.

Feelings of shame can lead to isolation and loneliness. When people get to the place where they need to ask for help to survive, the person on the other side of the desk at the social assistance office might be a neighbour or even a friend. Going to the food bank may mean seeing a fellow church member who volunteers their time. The lack of privacy was a theme that ran through many of the stories heard at the social audits. According to a man at the Kent County audit: "I am sometimes treated like a second-class citizen. I realize they are overloaded with clients. They could take the time to listen and hear what it is like being challenged and help find a solution. Each time I call I get a different caseworker, and it is very frustrating. You feel like a beggar."

ISARC's Huron County organizers suspected that stigma might keep people living with low incomes from speaking out. Service providers confirmed that many people do not ask for help for a simple reason: they are ashamed that they need it. In a culture that expects people to stand on their own, having to ask for welfare becomes a humiliating process. "Everybody knows."

As a single mother in Huron County admitted, "I had to swallow my pride numerous times going to food banks and calling churches."

During ISARC's social audit in rural communities, we repeatedly heard that this reluctance to seek assistance prompted many people with low incomes to work to give back to their communities, to volunteer to help provide the very services that they themselves might at times use or need. This volunteer work helps to preserve dignity, a sense of self. One disabled woman described how she formed a support group for people with the same disability. The local family health team was instrumental in helping out. "Even if there are little things we can do to help ourselves, we need to do them."

Despite the challenges faced by rural people living in poverty, those who worked on ISARC's social audit were continuously humbled and reminded of the resiliency that lies within our fellow human beings. One Niagara volunteer reflected on his experience of listening to the stories of rural people living in poverty: "I was encouraged and inspired by their determination to rise above, and their sense of humour."

A disabled woman in Huron County added, "That's the one part I need to work on every single day – is hope. It took a few years to put a smile back on my face."

□

In many respects the rural experience of poverty is similar to the urban. Living in poverty is humiliating, unhealthy, and claustrophobic.

Yet as the ISARC soundings showed, greater stigma and fewer transportation options are but two of the factors that make rural poverty different. Many rural people exhibit an independent spirit that makes it harder for them to ask for help. In small communities it can seem like everybody knows everybody. Needing to ask for welfare saddles people with a burden of shame and humiliation. Those providing services may be neighbours or friends. Yet we also heard many stories of people doing everything they can to better their communities. A woman impoverished by illness facilitates a support group for those who share her condition. A man on disability benefits works as a volunteer every day at the food bank to help others who face the same challenges.

When they opened up about their hardships and struggles, the people who spoke with us demonstrated tremendous courage. Are rural people independent-minded, determined to support themselves? Does their place in the community depend on being free from welfare's stigma? Will some choose to go hungry rather than face the shame of a handout? How different, really, is rural poverty?

"It is tempting to romanticize rural life as agricultural, pastoral, neighbourly and a place 'away from' crime, violence, pollution, and all the ills that have become associated, rightly or wrongly, with urban life," concluded the 2008 Senate Committee that investigated rural poverty. "While there is a great deal of truth in this romantic vision," the Committee stated, it serves to obscure how "historically and to this day, rural life has often been filled with hardship, danger, and sometimes despair."

A first glance around the leafy countryside that surrounds the House of Lazarus in Mountain might confirm the romantic impression of country life. But the growing need for food bank services confirms a different reality. And even as rural Ontario has always harboured much hardship, things have changed. There are no more one-room schoolhouses and far fewer mixed family farms. Things have become centralized and there is much talk of globalization as children head off to big, faraway schools and more and more farms are factory-scale operations. Some areas from Meaford and Brighton to Leamington and Simcoe are home for part of the year to migrant farmworkers from Mexico and the Caribbean who must pay into the employment insurance and Canada pension plans but cannot collect any benefits.

"Workers are unable to self-advocate for themselves for fear of repatriation," a worker with the temporary foreign worker program told us. "The rise in the number of 'illegal' workers has created a vulnerable subgroup."

The Senatorial group that looked into rural poverty included not just the likes of former NHL great Frank Mahovlich but also a young high-school student who acted as a recorder at the Huron County hearing.

"In the committee's hearings with the rural poor, those who work with the rural poor, and academics who study poverty, one consistent theme emerged," the Senators concluded. "Canada's income support policies are a tangle of confusing, often punitive and outdated rules that often impede rather than advance the cause of poverty reduction."

"We live in a very developed, wealthy country where there are great opportunities, far more opportunities than in the world's countless impoverished countries," said the student volunteer. "Yet people are not able to access these opportunities because of disabilities they can't heal or help. In such a medically advanced country known for its universal health care, those with disabilities should be able to gain access to the medications they need, regardless of their income. In such a developed country, they should not have to beg for decent shelter. They should not have to decide between keeping their son or daughter at home and receiving the support they need to get healthy."

17 Theological Reflections on Poverty

Bhante Saranapala, Sister Doryne Kirby, Rabbi Larry
Englander, and Imam Shafiq Hudda

> The only sane response [to persistent poverty] is paradoxically a
> kind of schizophrenia: to put pressure on the government as if
> charity didn't exist and to engage in charitable work as if the gov-
> ernment didn't care. . . . Our ultimate aim remains to shape a soci-
> ety whose ideal is the elimination of poverty.
> – Dow Marmur, Rabbi Emeritus, Holy Blossom Temple, Toronto

FAITH COMMUNITIES HAVE LONG PROVIDED charitable services in
local communities, services that have helped people survive on low
incomes, that have helped to make their lives better. Yet the prophets,
traditions, leaders, and sacred books of these faiths have also called for
building a world in which all people have the means to live a decent and
secure life, in which they have the means both to have dignity and to be
treated with dignity. Faith communities see the essentials of life (food,
shelter, clothing, transportation, community) as the building blocks of
this world in which all people can both maintain their self-respect and
manage to care for their families. Poverty is a force that has destroyed
human dignity. Thus the persistence of poverty is an ethical and moral
dilemma that must be addressed, with deliberate speed, as a question of
the highest priority.

Bhante Saranapala, Sister Doryne Kirby, Rabbi Larry Englander, and
Imam Shafiq Hudda are four faith leaders who have walked with people
who are poor. They, like other participants in the ISARC audit, have not
only provided a social analysis of the poverty but also contemplated the
meaning of poverty's persistence. Here their theological reflections focus
on ways of discerning a faith-based response to the economic and social
suffering of adults and children in a wealthy Ontario.

Teachings as Tools: A Buddhist Perspective
Bhante Saranapala

Poverty is not something new to this hemisphere, let alone the world. Thousands, perhaps even tens of thousands, of women, men, and children suffer from conditions of poverty. Here I want to consider the Buddhist perspective on poverty and discuss ways of alleviating poverty.

Like other religions, Buddhism is sometimes criticized for its idealism. It certainly encourages a non-materialistic way of life and encourages its followers to invest in an internal richness. It is even obligatory for members of Buddhist monastic fraternities, like mine, to live in poverty, something akin to taking a perpetual vow of poverty in a Christian monastic sense. For Buddhist monks, it is canonical and is in line with the teaching of the Blessed One, who extolled the virtues of the spirit of poverty and non-detachment and admonished his disciples to live in a spirit of poverty.

According to Buddhism, human poverty springs from the lack of basic material needs or of the wherewithal to lead a decent life free from hunger, exposure, and disease. Buddhism recognizes the importance of such minimum human needs as essentials; Buddhism holds that these primary needs must of necessity be fulfilled for the sake of spiritual liberation. Buddha's Middle Path presupposes these basic requisites of survival and leads to the maintenance of a harmonious equilibrium of a healthy mind in a healthy body *(mens sana in corpore sano)* – a prerequisite to the Awakening of Enlightenment. Even in the monastic community – given to poverty – there is a certain criterion or benchmark, as a measure or level of living, below which a monastic fraternity or sorority should not be allowed to fall.

A Buddhist "renunciate" must conform to four standards to ensure survival: 1) food sufficient to alleviate hunger and maintain one's health, 2) clothing sufficient to be socially decent and to protect the body; 3) housing or shelter sufficient for enabling the person to cultivate the mind; and 4) health care sufficient to cure and prevent disease.

Providing for people's basic needs is enshrined in the U.N. Charter of Human Rights, and rich nations pay lip service to this objective. If practised in earnest, it can be one great solution to global poverty and many of the social ills that poverty brings in its train, such as poverty-induced crime, deprivation, and family dislocation.

Buddhism holds that poverty is a form of *Dukkha*, a Pali term often translated as suffering, which becomes meaningless in Buddhism when its corollary, "ending of Dukkha or suffering," is not factored in. The end purpose of Buddha's Path is ending Dukkha or suffering. The Buddha himself often emphasized that his teaching was "*Dukkha* – suffering – Ending Dukkha and How One Can Do It." An important element forming an integral part of ending Dukkha is the doctrine of non-attachment. Indeed, this is *a sine qua non*. Non-attachment serves to promote a simple, frugal, down-to-earth lifestyle that supports the virtue of *having less wants*. It encourages a lessening of the intrinsic desire to possess more and holds out the accumulation of possessions as a hindrance to happiness.

Buddhism proffers a code of ethical and moral conduct as a set of training principles for the practitioner. These principles are not to be embraced out of a sense of obedience or fear of some consequence, but embraced for the calming of the senses and the sake of uplifting one's own personal growth and mental stability. The practice of these training principles follows a logical sequence of spiritual growth absolutely necessary for attaining the final goal of Enlightenment. To that end, Buddhism teaches precepts for all levels of involvement, from the monastic community to lay practitioners.

These training principles are:

- not taking the life of (destroying) any living being – denoting respect for all forms of life equally – not only human life – denoting universal compassion;
- not taking that which is not given – denoting generosity at your capacity;
- not indulging in sexual misconduct – cognizant of the social and established norms of conduct for the good order of society;
- not uttering or resorting to false speech (lying, idle talk, gossip);
- not taking intoxicants that serve to alter brain function so that one cultivates awareness and remains alert.

An education through this fundamental framework of moral conduct, and a willingness to practise it, will help any person. If put into practice, these principles can help the rich and the poor alike. The framework can help to shift the dynamic of depression, confusion, or guilt often accompanied by poverty, empowering people to tap their inner creative energies for personal development.

However, all people need a helping hand from time to time – like someone who is in a dark cave finds the use of a flashlight helpful. Those who are experiencing misfortune need the help of others.

The West End Buddhist Cultural Centre has been lending a helping hand to the less fortunate in our area. We support local soup kitchens by sending our community children, youth, and adults to volunteer

time, resources, and material goods collected among themselves. Ines-
timable are the great benefits of this experience for the young minds in
their understanding of the human world that they live in and the compassionate teaching of the Buddha, which exhorts his disciples to associate with the wise and not with the foolish. This teaching need not be
taken literally, however, and it does not mean to segregate or discrimi-
nate against those whom we class as foolish.

In Buddhist terms, a fool can be a highly educated and eminently
placed individual in society. Associating with the foolish is a waste of
time and does not lead to positive results and can be an impediment to
one's progress. We are influenced by who we hang around with. When
we are around someone who is angry, we find it difficult to be calm and
happy. Likewise, when we are around someone who is happy and
upbeat, we can find our own mood being transformed into something
positive. When we visit a soup kitchen, we bring with us positive vibes
of love and caring, and we have seen this mood become contagious.

From time to time the issue of poverty comes up in discussions at
our temple. One member recently mentioned a time when he was homeless, and how what really pulled him out of his depression was the kindness and small acts of help he had received along the way. Looking back
with some satisfaction, we see that our temple's services, even in simple
things like providing a needy person or family with a place to sleep,
food to eat, medical care, and mental and spiritual support, have
wrought wonders in individuals and families and been instrumental in
restoring their self-esteem and sense of dignity and worth as human
beings. It is essential to meet a human being's basic needs for survival.

Perhaps one of the most interesting aspects of Buddhism, especially
with regard to poverty, is its emphasis on human potential, the enor-
mous capacity of the human person to put his or her mind to work.
Buddhism does not extol human poverty as an opportunity for the well-
to-do to do good. On the other hand, Buddhism does not condemn
riches either, if legitimately earned.

Buddhist scriptures and folklore exemplify enterprise, entrepreneur-
ship and business acumen, and gains made in business by legitimate
means. Buddha, recalling his past lives, pointed to an era in which he,
as an aspirant to Buddha-hood (*Bodhisatta*), was once a salesman with
a sales territory over which he presided. Another story tells of how the
Bodhisatta was born into a very poor family but seized the opportunity
after listening to a wise man and through judicious buying and selling
(of stocks) made quite a fortune to become one of the richest men of
that time, attracting the attention of the ruling monarch's pretty and

accomplished daughter, whom he married and lived with happily ever after.

The Buddhist teachings, then, can be used as tools to develop one's inherent potential. As a community, we have the responsibility to offer our resources, our time, our talents, our forgiveness, and our knowledge or spiritual understanding, all of which we have acquired without seeking any kind of reward.

A government in turn has the responsibility, as outlined by the Buddha, to practise the *Dasa-Raja-Dhamma*, the "Ten Duties of the King (RULER)," as a means of good governance to render an equitable, just society without poverty. The ten principles are:

1. Dana – generosity – the head of the state must practise charity. This person "should not have craving and attachment for wealth and property, but should give it away for the welfare of the people."
2. Sila – morality – the head of the state must be of a high and moral character. This person "should never destroy life, cheat, steal and exploit others, commit adultery, utter falsehood, or take intoxicating drinks."
3. Pariccaga – sacrifice – the head of the state should sacrifice everything for the good of the people. This person "must be prepared to give up all personal comfort, name and fame, and even his life, in the interest of the people."
4. Ajjava – honesty and integrity – the head of the state "must be free from fear and favor in the discharge of his duties, must be sincere in his intentions, and must not deceive the public."
5. Maddava – kindness and gentleness – the head of the state "must possess a genial temperament."
6. Tapa – austerity of habits – the head of the state "must lead a simple life, and should not indulge in a life of luxury. He must have self-control."
7. Akkodha – freedom from envy, ill-will, and enmity – the head of the state "should bear no grudge against anybody."
8. Avihimsa – non-violence – the head of the state "should harm nobody, should try to promote peace by avoiding and preventing war, and everything which involves violence and destruction of life."
9. Khanti – patience, forbearance, tolerance, understanding – the head of the state "should be able to bear hardships, difficulties, and insults without losing his temper."
10. Avirodha – non-opposition, non-obstruction – the head of the state "should not oppose the will of the people, should not obstruct any

measures that are conducive to the welfare of the people. In other words he should rule in harmony with his people."

I am happy to leave these thoughts with you. These are not my own ideas but those of Gautama Buddha, the Fully Awakened One, who expressed those norms of human salvation in compassion for the human race, for individuals and institutions slipping away, just as today, from their secure moorings of morality, stability, and peace.

May the rains come in good season for a rich harvest for all citizens; may the world be

Prosperous! Peaceful and harmonious! May the rulers of nations be righteous!

Seeking Solutions to Poverty: What Is the Christian Response?
Sister Doryne Kirby

The response is love – Christian or otherwise. And what, precisely, does that mean?

If we look at the situation of persistent poverty in Ontario, what is it we see? What repels us? Mostly what we see is the heart of those caught in the midst of the mire that is poverty. We can describe the physical poverty – and this happens all the time. Hungry children, teenagers, and adults, who are all without food, or have so little food that they think of little else. Or else they have minds bent on activities, however violent, that seek outlets from gnawing stomachs. How can we expect young people to find satisfaction in school, when they mingle with those who do not suffer from hunger pangs? These students are impeded from growing into a sense of their own dignity and importance.

What is the home environment of these hungering human persons in persistent poverty? True, not all of those caught in the despair of poverty will live in circumstances of disarray, or disastrous overcrowding, with dismal or diminished home furnishings. Yet the home environment will leave much to be desired. Are the children penalized and caught in a cauldron of nothingness? Do their environmental situations destroy their ability to feel good about themselves and life in general?

Love leads the way into seeing what is happening to the "person" of those caught in persistent poverty, and it urges us to move towards an alleviation of these situations.

Seeing this picture – which is more than just viewing the broad picture – is haunting, especially when we see and touch the very person affected by poverty. This is looking at reality! Yes, and it is difficult to reach out and embrace the effects of poverty that crush the minds and hearts of those caught in its all-empowering grip. It is difficult to see the ugliness of the violence that so often ensues.

All children and youth, especially those consumed in persistent poverty, crave role models. When people are disrespected, they find easy outlets in untoward behaviour. The hungry heart of a youthful braggart becomes resistant to kindly overtures and is hard to love.

Our middle-class contentment in the "status quo of plenty" can cause myopic vision. Even when we clearly see the physical effects of poverty, we can find it difficult to understand its painfully damaging effects. We complain and cry out at a lack of vigilance in the behaviour of those abandoned to persistent poverty and then remain lacklustre about the phenomenon, not seeing its origin or taking effective action to circumvent the harmful causes.

Love gives sight beyond ugly exteriors and hears – yes, love hears – the hungry cries of an abandoned heart yearning for acceptance.

It is impossible to fully understand the persistence of poverty in Ontario. How does it happen in Canada, in Ontario, that people like you and me are so resistant to taking the steps necessary to change attitudes and engage in appropriate action towards the elimination of persistent poverty? What steps are required?

Could we ask for open minds? Can we begin by suggesting that the persistent poor are not harbingers of their own misery or not just getting what they deserve for being lazy? How about looking into the personal investments that are often made to keep the poor in their place – in order to ensure me of my own personal prosperity?

Seeking solutions will involve assessments of personal responsibility. Does persistent poverty continue so that my own comforts and contentment can continue unabated?

Seeking solutions does involve making an honest assessment of situations. Good solutions will see the inner persons of the sisters and brothers in our world, all of them as loving creations of an all-embracing Creator God, desirous of a world in which justice and compassionate relationships can reign supreme.

Yes, solution seekers are honest enough to say – "Persistent poverty is wrong, is evil, and my personal integrity is on the line if I continue to contribute to its existence, its maintenance."

For Christians the following of Jesus is the ultimate awareness and model of response to knowing how our generous and giving God would have us care for the less fortunate, those unaware of their own integrity and wholeness.

Never give up! This is the key to seeking the elimination of the persistent poverty that nags at the essential goodness of the people of Ontario. We do not adequately help, not because we are inherently bad but just because we are inherently blind – for the most part. Selfishness and greed and the urge to power and domination jeopardize the ability to live in healthy relationships in society. Physically, psychologically, the poorest pay for our neglect. If we perpetuate poverty, we become spiritually and emotionally deprived.

So the journey continues for each of us – imbibing to the fullest the awareness of God's continued Presence in our midst, especially among all the poor of this world, both materially and psychologically.

The response, Christian or otherwise, can be summed up in the words of Dom Helder Camara, who once said, "When one dreams alone, it is only a dream. When we dream together, it is the beginning of reality."

See! Judge! Act! Peer into the world and be aware of God's Presence throughout the tiniest aspect of Creation. This mystery of Presence in myself, in the other, prompts us towards those actions respectful of a loving God. And the inevitability of the living out of such a reality will surely have a positive influence in lessening the situation of persistent poverty in Ontario.

A Rabbi's View: Changing Attitudes
Rabbi Larry Englander

For years now, ISARC has published reports on poverty and homelessness in Ontario. And for years now we have seen the numbers steadily increase. Food banks have sprung up throughout the province, and the client list grows longer each year. In Peel Region alone, from the time that a family places their name on the list for subsidized housing, they face a wait of approximately twenty-one years – enough time, if they are lucky, for one of their children to attain an apartment.

There are those who argue that we should not be alarmed at this state of affairs. After all, even the book of Deuteronomy (chapter 15) tells us that "the poor shall never cease out of the land." In fact, we may always find people who, for whatever reason, lack the coping skills to make ends meet and who will need the loving support of their community. And that is why our faith communities must continue to provide that support.

But if the very presence of the underprivileged does not alarm us, there is something else that should. It is the popular *attitude* towards "them" that we need to change. It is still a widely held opinion in our society that the poor are somewhat inferior human beings and therefore deserve the hardships that they face. It is widely accepted that politicians will make a list of promises to rectify the situation; and as soon as these politicians get into power we do not even expect them to keep those promises. It is widely assumed that our best policy is to make minor adjustments here and there to "the system," while we ignore the generations of women, men, and children who spend their lives without adequate food, shelter, and health care in a land that now experiences unprecedented wealth.

To bring about positive change in people's lives, we must also initiate a change in these conventional attitudes. Perhaps we can learn from a rabbi who lived in the early centuries of the Common Era. The Talmud records (*Berakhot* 58b):

> Rabbi Chana bar Hanilai had sixty bakers in his house day and night, baking for anyone who needed bread.... His doors were open to all four directions, and anyone who came in hungry would leave satisfied. In times when food was scarce, he would leave wheat and barley outside the door, so that anyone who was too embarrassed to come and take in the daytime could come unnoticed and take at night.

Rabbi Chana's attitude was markedly different from today's conventional wisdom. Instead of waiting for the need to reach crisis proportions, he acted *before* the need was even articulated. Would it be such an outlandish idea for our society to become proactive in our response to the poor and homeless? Can you imagine a time when we have more subsidized apartments available than there are people requesting them? More free food available at more locations throughout our neighbourhoods?

We might also dare to imagine that such a state of affairs would create a ripple effect. Scientific studies have already demonstrated that people living in poverty suffer in greater proportion from physical and mental disease. If our society helps more individuals to live in dignity, the result is that less people would land up in hospital with ailments caused by malnutrition. Prisons would have more room – some may even have to close – because there would be less temptation for people to resort to crime. And there would be an added bonus for everyone: because a government subsidy for an apartment costs less than a hospital bed or a prison cell, we would even experience a reduction in taxes.

Given that the resources are at our disposal, might this approach at least be worth a try? Rabbi Chana thought so. Maybe we can convince our politicians!

The Islamic Approach: Curing a Social Ill
Imam Shafiq Hudda

Islam believes strongly in the eradication of poverty, and has implemented a number of policies to achieve this goal, after recognizing its
existence, and offering solutions.

First of all, Islam regards poverty as a social ill, part of which can be
attributed to wealthy, capitalistic individuals who are greedy and do not
pay heed to the needs of the less fortunate. Imam Ali, the first Imam, or
Leader after Prophet Muhammad (peace be upon him and his family),
has been quoted as saying, *"If you see a hungry one, know that someone has snatched the food that was rightfully his."* This statement is not
simply referring to food specifically, but rather the fair, equitable distribution of wealth as a whole. Food is perhaps used symbolically here.
While Islam allows, in fact encourages, its followers to earn, collect,
and save wealth in permissible ways, it orders its adherents to ensure
that those around them are not hungry. The whole issue of giving charity means that one has to have sufficient from which one gives. Like any
ailment, poverty needs to be treated, and eventually cured. The society
as a whole is encouraged to participate in this struggle.

Secondly, on a practical level Islam strives to ensure that one is not
neglectful of what one's Lord expects. Imam Sadiq, the sixth Imam,
said, *"If your neighbour is going to sleep hungry and your own stomach
is satiated, do not consider yourself our follower* (Muslim)." This
hadith, or saying, did not mention whether the neighbour was Muslim,
Christian, atheist, polytheist, or anything else; rather, it considers the
hunger of any human in the neighbourhood. Since Muslims are spread
out in many areas of many countries, theoretically there should be no
poverty around them. A number of obligatory dues are required from
every Muslim, which in turn get distributed to those in need, in the
effort to eliminate poverty. One such tax is the Zakat, which Muslims
give from their income, regarded as a pillar of Islam. Following the
month of Ramadhan, the faithful must give three kilograms of the food
they consumed most during the year, or its cash equivalent, to be distributed locally among those in need, called Fitra, or Zakat-ul-Fitr. During the holy month itself, optional charities are given in large numbers,
since Muslims are hungry and thirsty during the daylight hours, and
experiencing first-hand what the poor go through regularly.

Lastly, the holy Prophet Muhammad (peace be upon him and his
family) did not only offer short-term solutions, but also encouraged
long-term plans. In certain cases, when a destitute companion would
come and ask for charity, the Prophet would give him some aid and

then suggest a business that the companion could consider opening. He was also known to provide modest start-up capital to many companions, borrowing the amount from others interest-free, and helping the needy get back on their feet. Prophet Muhammad was known to encourage his companions to employ those without jobs in their fields or on their farms, and for trade expeditions. The theory has been "Give a man a fish, feed him for a day; teach a man to fish, feed him for a lifetime." Perpetual, or even temporary, poverty is something that Islam abhors, and has made efforts to eradicate from the society. For the sake of humanity we must pray for, as well as strive for, the realization of this goal.

18 A Pebble in the Shoe

> The problems in rich countries are not caused by the society not being rich enough but by the scale of material differences between people in each society being too big.
> – Richard Wilkinson and Kate Pickett, *The Spirit Level: Why Equality Is Better for Everyone*, 2009

"SCRUPLES" IS THE NAME OF A CANADIAN-INVENTED board game involving questions that raise tricky moral dilemmas. Since its introduction in 1984, some seven million copies of Scruples have been sold. Contestants puzzle over thought-provoking questions such as: "The teacher asks if you wrote your son's book report. Your son claimed he did it, but the teacher is right. Do you admit it?"

A scrupulous person is someone who steps back and thinks carefully about what is morally right. This is what one of Canada's most eloquent elders was getting at in 2010 just as ISARC's social audits were in full swing. Ursula Franklin discussed the way in which her Quaker forebears in eighteenth-century Britain used "scrupling" in a crucial advocacy campaign of the day. It was not a game, but a fundamental moral issue: should slavery continue to exist?

Franklin – metallurgist, pacifist, and social critic – talked about the Quakers' long campaign to convince their fellow citizens that it was morally reprehensible to own other human beings and have the legal right to flog and brand them. The Quaker campaign to put an end to the slave trade and slavery entailed bringing people together to confront uncomfortable ethical and political issues with a view to charting a new course.

This was also what ISARC did when we organized hearings that offered low-income people the chance to tell their stories. For far too long, far too many people in this province have faced a daily grinding struggle to obtain enough decent food and maintain adequate shelter. For some twenty-five years now ISARC has been trying to convince the politicians and the rest of the population that tolerating this situation is a disgrace – particularly when humankind has obtained such a high level of material and technical accomplishment. In the course of our hearings, a woman who had come to Canada from Africa described her surprise at seeing homelessness in downtown Kitchener. The region was overflowing with new wealth generated by its computer industries, most notably RIM's Blackberry. "Why such poverty in a country with such wealth?"

Our efforts hearken back to the Latin origin of the word "scruple." A *scrupus* was a sharp stone or pebble. The word was used by the Roman philosopher and orator Cicero, who employed it figuratively – a pebble in a shoe is the cause of nagging unease until the cause is removed. The Latin word *scrupulus* is defined as "uneasiness, anxiety, pricking on conscience." Perhaps in some modest way ISARC has been a sharp pebble in the shoe of Ontario's political class and, more generally, a constant reminder to the wider body politic. Scrupling.

At the end of our previous book (*Lives Still in the Balance)* in this series, we discussed the urgent need for a shift in policy *and* in public attitude. We have seen some signs of a shift in public policy in Ontario: an Ontario *Poverty Reduction Act* and an accompanying strategy; some tax-based measures to help parents who are raising children in poverty; increases in the minimum wage; a marginal improvement to labour standards enforcement and social assistance rates.

Still, these tentative baby steps have not been nearly enough to make a substantial difference in the lives of marginalized people. What we need is a great leap forward.

Faith communities have long been committed to the welfare of the vulnerable among us. We have started meal programs, set up hospitals before health care became available to all, helped to organize housing co-operatives and non-profit shelter initiatives during the years when government was committed to affordable housing. Having assisted in securing support for emergency food assistance, we know that a well of public sympathy exists for the plight of the poor. Indeed, food banks have become so popular that they are the default charities for groups seeking to do good work in the community. Corporations like them too. One courier company runs a Tackle Hunger campaign by donating the player's weight in food every time a Canadian Football League quarterback is "sacked" – tackled before he can throw the ball. But we also know that tossing a few cans into a food drive bag is an easy way of assuaging our consciences, of convincing ourselves that we have somehow done our bit for the less fortunate.

While faith communities provided what they assumed would be temporary survival services, such as Out of the Cold programs, food

banks, soup kitchens, and emergency shelters, these arrangements
became permanent, draining the resources of faith groups and other
charities. Volunteers grew exhausted. The volunteer pool shrank. Faith
leaders watched their own resources dwindling and saw ever more
clearly the need for stronger advocacy efforts.

Public support for the poor remains a mile wide but an inch deep.
Our most vulnerable neighbours remain easy targets for politicians
seeking to take advantage of residual resentments against the poor by
attempting to score cheap political points by poor-bashing. Too often
some of us regard the poor as a form of subspecies or, at best, as victims. Our individualism, our belief that "it could never happen to me,"
can easily prevent us from acting in solidarity with poor people. As we
have seen in the preceding pages, this habit is wearing thin as indebtedness rises, savings shrink, and the job market fails to generate work that
provides living wages and basic benefits.

One such benefit is the dental care that we all need but that government refuses to inaugurate as part of public health-care provision. In
2007 the provincial Liberal Party, campaigning for re-election, promised
to start a program of dental care for low-income people. Yet just as
ISARC was holding its 2010 social audit, Health Minister Deb Matthews
– formerly the government's poverty reduction champion – was
announcing that there was no money available for dental care for
Ontario's half-million working poor. Declaring that it would be "wonderful" to provide basic dental care to adults working in precarious
jobs, Matthews announced that the $135 million earmarked in 2007 for
these people would instead go to their children.

"We are facing a lot of challenges," she said. "We're focusing on
children and I'm excited. I think it is a big step in the right direction."[1]

Big steps or tentative baby steps? Clearly, no great leap forward –
particularly when three programs already exist to meet children's dental
needs. There is little to assist adults beyond dental emergency programs,
whose main focus is pain reduction, often through tooth extraction.
There is no money for dentures. In one chilling report from our audits,
people did succeed in finding dentures. One woman from a large
Ontario city lost her dentures, and Ontario Works would not replace
them. But she needed teeth, and she found out about one grisly way of
obtaining them. She went on the black market to obtain the dentures
from a funeral home. The facilitator of the social audit was so shocked
that we double-checked the story through other sources. We confirmed
that some people on social assistance have indeed been obtaining dentures through funeral homes.

ISARC is worried about what might be called the "politics of poverty." The provincial government elected in 2003 chose health care and education – not poverty – as the two areas in which to invest the proceeds of a red hot economy that would continue for another five years. Unlike those areas, the issue of poverty did not appear to be a direct concern of the broad middle class that is nevertheless feeling increasingly insecure because of mounting debt and longer working hours. This broad middle class is made up of people who tend to vote. The poor remain a minority, invisible to most of the population, even though poverty costs us all.[2]

Moreover, the poor are a minority that tends *not* to vote, such is the cynical fatalism about the chances of change. This was borne out in the Durham social audit, when five municipal councillors reflected on social service delivery, downloading, and the responsibilities of cities. All of them agreed that social services do not play a political role – that they neither help them nor harm them come election time. And, they added, the poor, particularly the people who live in apartment buildings, do not vote. For their part, one low-income man in Durham declared, "Politicians talk to you for your vote – all they want is money."

Because the poor are a disengaged minority, governments find it easier to disregard their needs, no matter how urgent those needs may be – like people whose remaining front teeth are so grey and soft that they cannot get job interviews.

☐

For social justice campaigners, including ISARC, advocacy efforts are complex and difficult. We have not been blameless in perpetuating poverty. Ever since the House of Commons famously – and unanimously – voted in 1989 to end child poverty by the year 2000, we have too often focused our advocacy efforts on poor children. A child is innocent, surely not the author of her or his own plight. A child simply had the bad luck to be born into a poor family, or to have a sole-support mother, or a disabled father, or to suffer from fetal alcohol system disorder. It is easier to scruple on behalf of children by showcasing outrageous levels of child poverty than it is to scruple on behalf of working-age adults who are unemployed or disabled or both. As a result, Ontario poverty reduction policy has become skewed in the direction of child tax credits and child benefit programs that do nothing for people whose children have left home or who do not happen to have children. It brings to mind that nefarious

Victorian-era distinction between the deserving and undeserving poor (see chapter 6).

Many of the people who told ISARC their stories suffer from the stigma associated with poverty. They are excluded from mainstream life. When we took the pulse of Ontario's communities in 2010, many of our informants – mainly mothers – spoke of how hard it was for them to tell their children that there were a lot of things that they just could not have because those items were simply unaffordable. This is not just in the case of life's necessities, such as nutritious food. It is also a matter of the latest running shoes or a particular kind of knapsack for school or a school trip – things that *everyone else* has.

Many people in Ontario, as in other rich places, are preoccupied with the flash and grab of consumer culture. We live in a must-have world, surrounded by things for sale. We are inundated from infancy with advertising messages telling us that what we have says something important about who we are.

Related to the notion of possessions as markers of merit are issues of pride and shame, the feelings that people have when they find themselves lingering for the first time outside the food bank. For adults who have never thought that they would find themselves in this situation, it is no less hurtful than it is for children who can't go on a school trip or have that latest brand-name bauble. Or who have no computer at home.

According to one recent study of the social epidemiology of fractured societies: "When we talk about 'hurt feelings' or a 'broken heart' we recognize the connection between physical pain and the social pain caused by the breaking of close social bonds, by exclusion and ostracism."[3]

These authors show conclusively that living in countries that are unequal tends to weaken community life. Moreover, Ontario is becoming less egalitarian all the time[4] – and the more unequal a society is, the more troubled it is. The rate of mental illness is five times higher in the most unequal societies compared to the most egalitarian. Rates of imprisonment are five times higher. Clinical obesity is six times higher.[5]

In 2010, just as Ontario was launching its much-touted extension of full-day kindergarten (see chapter 14), a report by People for Education revealed the alarming levels of private funding for public schools in a province that has no policy on parental fees and corporate involvement in schools. A Niagara mother had written to the local school board when she received a form about "mandatory" fees for student activities that, she learned, included access to the school library. Marion Battersby learned that the fee can be waived for financial reasons, but that parents had to take the initiative to apply for this exception. People for Education found that such fees lead to "exclusion or built-in inequity." The organization added, "The increased reliance on fees and fundraising inevitably leads to a system of 'have' and have-not' schools."[6]

☐

One of the obscene paradoxes of our times is that we are ready, willing, and able to produce far too much "stuff." All of this amounts to an endless chain that starts in the Chinese factory and continues to the suburban mall before ending at the yard sale and the garbage dump. We keep on doing this in the belief that endless growth will somehow solve all our problems. It will not. On a global basis, the richest fifth of the population consumes four-fifths of the planet's resources. Our contributor Armine Yalnizyan points out that between 1981 and 2005 Ontario's economy grew by 310 per cent – from $131 billion to almost $538 billion. It is four times bigger than it was in 1981. Adjusted for inflation, the "real" economy more than doubled in size.[7]

But this fantastic economic growth has not diminished the existence of poverty. The level of poverty has remained stubbornly high. The stories in this book add a human face to the stark numbers. In a place of plenty, we have failed to democratize prosperity.

As faith communities, we question both growing inequality and the need for an infinite recurrence of growth that threatens life on a planet where nature's bounty is so clearly finite. Endless growth does not – as so many economists and politicians insist it will – trickle down to those most in need. Ecological footprint analysis compares the human impact on the planet with the amount of land and water that nature has to offer. One theorist of the ecological footprint, Mathis Wackernagel, argues that if present growth and demand trends continue we will need the equivalent of two Earths by the late 2030s.[8]

Persistent poverty amidst unsustainable overabundance makes no sense. Poverty persists in part because of the belief that, if the economy just continues to grow, everyone will benefit. Economist John Kenneth Galbraith described this conventional wisdom of trickle-down economics as "the doctrine that if the horse is amply fed with oats, some will pass through to the road for the sparrows."[9] This doctrine may be conventional, but it is surely not wise. It must be challenged on a moral and ethical basis.

Love and justice have never been "trickle-down" virtues. They are values that both individuals and society must address. In Buddhism,

Christianity, Islam, and Judaism, government, rulers, and the people are required to seek justice and compassion for all in the land (see chapter 17). All adults require enough food, safe and adequate housing, and the ability to care for dependants. Visionary faith traditions emphasize a combination of compassion and justice to promote human dignity.

Back in the eighteenth century, when Quakers in Britain were scrupling about the morality of slavery, they were also challenging the way in which people suffering from mental illness were being treated. In 1796 retired Quaker tea merchant William Tuke opened the York Retreat, where people with psychiatric problems found an environment that ran against the conventional wisdom of the day. Back at the dawn of the industrial capitalist era, conventional wisdom about dealing with mental illness prescribed squalor and harsh punishment. The Quakers believe that there is "that of God" in all of us, and the Retreat offered a quiet and supportive place sympathetic to the needs of people with mental illness. William Tuke's grandson would later describe the underlying philosophy as "moral treatment."

The moral of the story is as clear and uncomplicated as it is timeless. The way in which we treat our most vulnerable neighbours – including, as our social audit so often heard, people suffering from mental illness – speaks volumes about the very nature of our society. Ethically and morally, a society is judged by how it treats its most vulnerable and marginalized members.

ISARC's latest social audit is based on the real-life experiences of what we call Ontario's poverty experts. Their stories and insights show that we have a long way to go before we can claim with any honesty that we are applying moral treatment in dealing with the least fortunate among us. All too often their lives are fractured not only by the sheer physical need for food and shelter but also by stigma and fear: stigma that comes from not being able to fit in based on how you should supposedly look and what you should have in a society that places a twisted premium on commodities; fear that yet another threatening government letter will result in the loss of a paltry stipend that is already not enough to support a dignified life.

Ursula Franklin was born in Germany and spent World War II in a Nazi work camp because her mother was a Jew. A lifelong pacifist, she describes peace as the presence of justice and the absence of fear. This book is a firm continuation of our own twenty-three-year scrupling effort. It is our hope that the voices of the real poverty experts will help to bring this sort of peace to those who have been neglected for such a long time.

Acknowledgements

Persistent Poverty: Voices from the Margins could not have been written without the support of many people and groups.

Most importantly, ISARC appreciated the courage and strength of people with low incomes who shared their experiences and perspectives. Their voices were the audit. In this book, to maintain their anonymity, we have not used their real names. ISARC was thankful that local changes to address poverty began even as these voices were being heard by local politicians, civic leaders, and rapporteurs from the faith communities.

Politicians, social service staff, health-care professionals, and volunteers added their voices to the audit to amplify the systemic issues that keep people and communities from breaking the cycle of poverty in Ontario. All participants energized ISARC and its faith communities to maintain the mandate to eliminate poverty in Ontario.

Funders of the 2010 Social Audit included:

- Assembly of Catholic Bishops of Ontario
- Atkinson Foundation
- Daly Foundation of the Sisters of Service
- Rick and Nancy Martin (Waterloo Region)
- Mennonite Savings and Credit Union
- The Redemptorists
- St. Vincent de Paul Society
- Sisters of Providence of St. Vincent de Paul (Kingston)
- Sisters of St. Joseph (London)
- Solel Congregation of Mississauga

Local organizations and faith groups supported the 2010 social

audit through staff time, use of facilities, and finances. The extent of
these contributions was not recorded. Although ISARC was able to provide financial support for people with low incomes to attend the social
audit forum on June 2, 2010, a number of local organizations provided
the transportation that made the forum even more successful.

Hearing Sites and local convenors:

Barrie-Orillia	Laurie van den Hurk & Jody Maltby
Belleville	John Brisebois
Brantford	JoAnne Dubois
Chatham-Kent	Jim Paddon
Cornwall	Michelle Gratton
Durham Region	Ted Glover
Halton-Burlington-Oakville	Colleen Sym
Hamilton	Diedre Pike and Colleen Sym
Huron County	Alexandra Beasse
Kingston	Jamie Swift
London	Joan Atkinson & Susan Eagle
Mississauga-Peel-Brampton	Larry Englander & Donna McBride
Mountain	Pauline Pratt
Niagara	Gracia Janes
North Bay	Tawnia Healey
Ottawa	Joe Gunn
Ottawa Valley–Renfrew	Lyn Smith
Saulte Ste. Marie	Jill Hewgill
Toronto Central	Bruce Voogd
Toronto East	Murray MacAdam
Toronto West	Bruce Voogd
Waterloo Region	Brice Balmer, Greg DeGroot Maggetti, Dina Etmanski, Michael Hackbusch, Janet Howitt, Cheryl Ives
Windsor	Adam Vasey
York Region	Yvonne Kelly & Thomas Pearson

Reports from previous community studies were received from Sarnia
and Parry Sound.

Each of these local community audits required significant time from
the convenors and local organizations, plus extensive use of the convenors' networks. The extent of the local involvement was significant
because each audit had convenors, facilitators, recorders, and rapporteurs.

Although ISARC staff and volunteers worked to form more connections in Ontario's Northern communities and with Aboriginal peoples, few audit hearings resulted. ISARC did not have the monies, staff time, and connections to conduct hearings in these areas. This year the social audit did include significant hearings in Ontario's rural communities. Poverty in Ontario has never been only an urban phenomenon. ISARC will plan to have future social audits become even more inclusive of Ontario's peoples.

Faith group members of Interfaith Social Assistance Reform Coalition include:

- Anglican Church of Canada
- Assembly of Catholic Bishops of Ontario
- Baptist Convention of Ontario and Quebec
- Buddhist Community of Greater Toronto
- Canadian Council for Reform Judaism
- Canadian Council of Imams
- Canadian Hindu Heritage Centre
- Canadian Islamic Congress
- Canadian Jewish Congress
- Canadian Religious Conference (Ontario Region Catholic Congregations)
- Canadian Unitarian Council
- Canadian Unitarians for Social Justice
- Council of Canadian Hindus
- Darchei Noam Reconstructionist Synagogue
- Evangelical Lutheran Church in Canada (Eastern Synod)
- Islamic Humanitarian Service
- Mennonite Central Committee, Ontario
- Ontario Coalition for Social Justice
- Pentecostal Assemblies of Canada
- Presbyterian Church in Canada
- The Salvation Army
- Society of Friends (Quakers)
- St. Vincent de Paul Society
- Toronto Board of Rabbis
- United Church of Canada.

These ISARC members provided the base funding for the coalition; many raised additional monies for the 2010 social audit. The ISARC steering committee included representatives from these faith groups; this steering committee made decisions about ISARC's staffing, work, and projects. Since September 2008 ISARC has been a project of the Water-loo Lutheran Seminary in Waterloo, Ontario; the seminary staff provided financial and supportive services.

The social audit tool kit was developed by Alexandra Beasse, who also drafted this book's chapter on rural poverty. She assembled the tool kit (available at www.isarc.ca) with support from Brice Balmer, Michael Maher, and the ISARC steering committee.

Finally, *Persistent Poverty* could not have taken shape without the steadfast encouragement and assistance of Murray MacAdam, the principal author of *Lives in the Balance* and *Lives Still in the Balance*. His wise counsel has been invaluable.

Notes

Introduction: The Work of Hundreds of People

1 *The Globe and Mail*, Aug. 2, 2010.

2 For more information on the 2010 audit's process, hearing sites and convenors, and faith group members, see the Acknowledgements.

3 For details of the U.N. human rapporteur model, see the 2010 Social Audit Tool Kit <www.isarc.ca>.

1: "As Sharp As You Could Cut Them"

1 Davies is quoted in Doug Fetherling, *A Little Bit of Thunder: The Strange Inner Life of the Kingston Whig-Standard* (Toronto: Stoddart, 1993), p.37; Lower is quoted in Jamie Swift, *Wheel of Fortune: Work and Life in the Age of Falling Expectations* (Toronto: Between The Lines, 1995), p.48.

2 ISARC, *Our Neighbours' Voices: Will We Listen?* (Toronto: Lorimer, 1998), pp.43–44.

3 "Ontario Passes Historic Poverty Reduction Act," Newsroom (Government of Ontario), May 6, 2009 <http://news.ontario.ca/mcys/en/2009/05/ontario-passes-historic-poverty-reduction-act.html>.

4 *Canadian Jewish News*, March 26, 2009.

5 Andrew Jackson and Sylvain Schetagne, "Is EI Working for Canada's Unemployed? Analyzing the Great Recession," Technical paper, Canadian Centre for Policy Alternatives, January 2010.

6 Armine Yalnizyan, Progressive Economics Forum, June 24, 2010 <http://www.progressive-economics.ca/2010/06/24/lone-parent-success-story-not-because-of-tough-love>.

7 René Morissette, "Earnings in the Last Decade," *Perspectives*, February 2008, Statistics Canada Cat. no. 75–001-X.

8 Armine Yalnizyan, "Ontario's Growing Gap," Canadian Centre for Policy Alternatives (CCPA), 2007.

2: Back to the Future? The Choice Is Ours

1 David Croll, "Poverty in Canada," Address to the Empire Club of Canada, Toronto, Jan. 27, 1972. All of the Croll citations here come from this speech.

2 Using Statistics Canada's Low-Income Cut-Offs (LICOs). See tables at <http://www.statcan.gc.ca/pub/75–202-x/75–202-x2008000-eng.htm>. To date, the LICO is the "golden standard" for measuring poverty in Canada, although there is no official, government-sanctioned measure of poverty.

3 Dave Bidini, "Heat Doesn't Make Homelessness Better," *National Post* (Toronto), July 10, 2010.

4 Other nations' information is from Janet C. Gornick and Markus Jäntti, "Child Poverty in Upper-Income Countries: Lessons from the Luxembourg Income Study," in *From Child Welfare to Child Well-Being: An International Perspective on Knowledge in the Service of Policy Making*, ed. Sheila B. Kamerman, Shelley Phipps, and Asher Ben-Arieh, vol. 1, Children's Well-Being: Indicators and Research Series (Dordrecht and New York: Springer, 2010). Canadian information is from Statistics Canada, Table 202–0802, Persons in Low Income.

5 Hugh Mackenzie, *A Soft Landing: Recession and Canada's Highest 100 Paid CEOs* (Ottawa: Canadian Centre for Policy Alternatives, January 2010); and Mackenzie, *The Great CEO Pay Race: Over Before It Begins* (Ottawa: Canadian Centre for Policy Alternatives, December 2007).

6 Armine Yalnizyan, *The Rich and the Rest of Us: The Changing Face of Canada's Growing Gap* (Ottawa: Canadian Centre for Policy Alternatives, 2007).

7 Statistics Canada, "Income in Canada," Catalogue no. 75–202-X.

8 Michael Ornstein, *Ethno-Racial Inequality in Toronto: Analysis of the 1996 Census* (Toronto: Institute for Social Research, York University, March 2000); and Grace-Edward Galabuzi, *Canada's Economic Apartheid: The Social Exclusion of Racialized Groups in the New Century* (Toronto: Canadian Scholars' Press, 2006).

9 All data from Statistics Canada, Labour Force Survey.

10 Ontario Association of Food Banks, *In the Midst of the Storm*, October 2009, Toronto; Daily Bread Food Bank, *Who's Hungry 2009*, Toronto.

11 René Morissette, "Earnings in the Last Decade," Statistics Canada, Catalogue no. 75–001-X, *Perspectives*, February 2008, Ottawa.

12 Canadian Labour Congress, *Recession Watch*, vol. 1, March 2009.

13 Armine Yalnizyan, "The Temporary Recovery," Canadian Centre for Policy Alternatives, Ottawa, April 12, 2010.

14 Armine Yalnizyan, "The Problem of Poverty Post-Recession," Canadian Centre for Policy Alternatives, Ottawa, August 2010.

15 All data are drawn from Statistics Canada, "Income in Canada," Catalogue no. 75–202-X.

3: Working Harder Is Hardly Working

1 Leah F. Vosko, *Managing the Margins: Gender, Citizenship, and the International Regulation of Precarious Employment* (Oxford: Oxford University Press. 2010), p.2.

2 Workers' Action Centre, *Working on the Edge*, Toronto, 2007, pp.40–41.

3 Ibid., p.15.

4: Precarious Work: How Lax Employment Standards Perpetuate Poverty

1 Workers' Action Centre, *Working on the Edge*, Toronto, 2007.

2 Statistics Canada, "Study: Quality of Employment in the Canadian Immigrant Labour Market," *The Daily*, Nov. 23, 2009.

3 Annette Bernhardt, Heather Boushey, Laura Dresser, and Chris Tilly, eds., *The Gloves Off Economy: Workplace Standards at the Bottom of America's Labor Market* (Ithaca, N.Y.: Cornell University Press, 2008).

4 Ontario's union density is below the Canadian average of 31 per cent. Statistics Canada, Labour Force Historical Review 2008, Table Cd3T09an, Cat. no. 71F0004XCB, 2009.

5 For example, only 22 per cent of unemployed workers in Toronto receive employment insurance benefits. Benefits are only 55 per cent of former earnings. For a discussion of problems with EI, see, for instance, "Time for a Fair Deal, Report of the Task Force on Modernizing Income Security for Working-Age Adults," Toronto, May 2006, p.21 <www.torontoalliance.ca/tcsa_initiatives/income_security>.

6 Statistics Canada, "Low Income Lines: 2008–2009" <http://www.statcan.gc.ca/pub/75f0002m/2010005/tbl/tbl02-eng.htm>.

7 Sheila Block, "Ontario's Growing Gap: The Role of Race and Gender," Growing Gap Series, Canadian Centre for Policy Alternatives, Ottawa, June 2010, p.5.

8 In 2008 there were 371,533 firms. Statistics Canada, Canadian Business Patterns Database, December 2008, "Number of Establishments by Type and Region: December 2008 Canadian Economy (NAICS 11–91)."

9 See Mark Thomas, *Regulating Flexibility: The Political Economy of Employment Standards* (Montreal and Kingston: McGill-Queen's University Press, 2009); Ron Saunders and Patrice Dutil, "New Approaches in Achieving Compliance with Statutory Employment Standards," Canadian Policy Research Network, 2005 <http://www.cprn.org/doc.cfm?doc=1271&l=en>; and Leah F. Vosko, ed., *Precarious Employment: Understanding Labour Market Insecurity in Canada* (Montreal and Kingston: McGill-Queen's University Press, 2006).

10 Harry Arthurs, *Fairness at Work: Federal Labour Standards for the 21st Century* (Ottawa: Federal Labour Standards Review, 2006).

11 Ontario Ministry of Labour, "Ontario Helping Live-in Caregivers," press release, Oct. 21, 2009 <http://news.ontario.ca/mol/en/s009/10/ontario-helping-live-in-caregivers.html>.

12 Human Resources Development Canada, *Evaluation of Federal Labour*

Standards (Phase 1) Final Report, Ottawa, 1997, p.41; 2005 Statistics Canada Federal Jurisdiction Workplace survey of employment practices, cited in Harry Arthurs, *Fairness at Work: Federal Labour Standards for the 21st Century* (Ottawa: Federal Labour Standards Review, 2006), p.192; Workers' Action Centre, *Working on the Edge*, p.46.

13 These figures are not adjusted for inflation and therefore understate the decline in funding. Data derived from Ministry of Labour, Historical Funding – Operations, 1997–98 to 2006–07, April 16, 2007 (on file with author); Labour Force Survey, 2006, Employees by Industry and Union Coverage, 2006 annual averages; and Ministry of Labour, *Annual Report of 2007–08*, July 8, 2008, ISSN 1718–682X, and Statistics Canada, Labour Force Survey, Table 282–0054.

14 Some of these workers may be exempted from overtime hours of work provisions. Statistics Canada, "Paid or Unpaid Overtime," The Canadian Labour Market at a Glance, Nov. 11, 2008; Statistics Canada 2007 average hourly wage ($19.13) x 9 hours (average hours of overtime worked) x 52 weeks x Statistics Canada January 2009 total employment (16,982,000) x 10% = $15,203,712,888 straight time wages + premium pay (plus 50%) = $22 billion: from Aaron Rousseau, "Overview of Overtime in Canada," *Employment & Labour*, March 18, 2009, Lang Michener, LLP <http://www.langmichener.ca/index.cfm?fuseaction=content.contentDetail& ID=10517&tlD=244>.

15 Saunders and Dutil, "New Approaches in Achieving Compliance."

16 Bill 68, *An Act to Promote Ontario as Open for Business by Amending or Appealing Certain Acts*, First Reading, May 17, 2010 <http://www.ontla.on.ca/bills/bills-files/39_Parliament/Session2/b068.pdf>.

17 Chris Bentley, "Statement to the Legislature Regarding 60-hour Work Week in Ontario," Legislative Assembly, *Legislative Debates* (Hansard), 38th Parl., 1st Session, April 26, 2004.

18 Workers' Action Centre, *Working on the Edge*.

19 For fuller discussions of this in Ontario, see Workers' Action Centre, *Working on the Edge*; Judy Fudge, "Reconceiving Employment Standards Legislation: Labour Law's Little Sister and the Feminization of Labour," *Journal of Law and Social Policy* 7 (1991), pp.73–89; and in the United States, see Bernhardt et al., *Gloves Off Economy*; Vosko, *Precarious Employment*; Saunders and Dutil, *"New Approaches in Achieving Compliance"*; Cynthia Cranford, Leah F. Vosko, and Nancy Zukewich, "Precarious Employment in the Canadian Labour Market: A Statistical Portrait," *Just Labour* 3 (2003).

For further information, see Workers' Action Centre <www.workersactioncentre.org>.

5: Ontario Works: How Did This Happen to Me?

1 See Bank of Canada Inflation Calculator <www.bankofcanada.ca/en/rates/inflation_calc.html>.

2 *Time for a Fair Deal: Report of the Task Force on Modernizing Income*

Security for Working Age Adults <www.torontoalliance.ca/MISWAA_Report
.pdf>.

3 *The Globe and Mail*, April 10, 2007.

6: The Disorienting Disability Support Maze

1 ALPHA (Association of Local Public Health Agencies), letter to Dalton
McGuinty, March 13, 2009 <http://www.alphaweb.org/sdoh.asp>.

2 ODSP Action Coalition, "Telling Our Stories: Disability Should Not Equal
Poverty," July 2010 <http://www.odspaction.ca/>.

7: The Affordable Housing Deficit: Out of the Cold

1 Homelessness and Housing Umbrella Group, Report Card 2010 <http://
www.hhug.ca/newsDetail.aspx?id=30>.

2 "Cost Effectiveness of Eviction Prevention Programs," Research Highlight
<http://www.winnipegrentnet.ca/resource-directory/resource/document/file/
cmhc%20eviction%20prevent%20summary1.pdf>.

8: Housing Strategy on the Brink: The Time Has Come

1 See the HNO Stable and Affordable.com website <http://stableandaffordable
.com>.

2 Fiscal 2008 is the last year that Statistics Canada released its Government
Revenues and Expenditures database. The per capita calculations are by the
Wellesley Institute based on GRE numbers and Statistics Canada population
information. Details are in the Wellesley Institute report *Precarious Housing
in Canada: Setting the Foundation for a National Housing Plan* (Toronto,
2010). The report is available at the website <www.wellesleyinstitute.com>.
For other data in this paragraph, see <http://www.onpha.on.ca/AM/Tem-
plate.cfm?Section=Waiting_Lists_2010>; <http://www.cmhc-schl.gc.ca/en/
corp/about/cahoob/data/data_013.cfm>; and <http://www.auditor.on.ca/en/
reports_en/en09/312en09.pdf>.

3 See chapter 3.12 on social housing <http://www.auditor.on.ca/en/reports_
2009_en.htm>.

4 There are numerous resources on the health impact of insecure housing and
homelessness. The opening chapter of the Wellesley Institute's *Precarious Housing in Canada* includes a listing of current and recent research. See also Canadian Institute of Health Information, *Housing and Population Health*, research
synthesis <http://secure.cihi.ca/cihiweb/products/HousingPopHealth_e.pdf>.

5 See, for instance, TD Economics' Affordable Housing in Canada
<http://www.td.com/economics/special/house03.pdf>; Multi-Faith Alliance
to End Homelessness <http://www.mfateh.ca/>; and Federation of Canadian
Municipalities housing information <http://www.fcm.ca/english/View.asp
?mp=1237&x=1119>.

6 Statistics Canada, Census of Canada 2006; Canada Mortgage and Housing
Corporation, Housing in Canada On-Line.

7 Statistics Canada Survey of Household Spending; Canada Mortgage and
Housing Corporation, Canadian Housing Observer data tables.

8 See, for instance, RBC Economics Housing Affordability <http://www.rbc .com/economics/market/pdf/house.pdf>.

9 Public Accounts of Ontario <http://www.fin.gov.on.ca/en/budget/paccts/ 2009/>.

10 Ibid.

11 See ⟨http://www.infrastructureontario.ca/en/loan/housing/index.asp⟩.

12 See the HNO Stable and Affordable.com website <http://www.stableandaf-fordable.com/sites/default/files/HNO%205%20Tests%20for%20Success %20April%2019.pdf>.

9: The Cost of Hunger: Food Security and Health Issues

1 Dietitians of Canada, "Individual and Household Food Insecurity in Canada: Position of Dietitians of Canada," *Canadian Journal of Dietetic Practice and Research* 66 (2005):43–46 <http://www.dietitians.ca/news/ downloads/Food_Insecurity_position.pdf>.

2 Food Banks Canada, *Hunger Count 2009: A Comprehensive Report on Hunger and Food Bank Use in Canada, and Recommendations for Change,* Toronto, 2009
<http://foodbankscanada.ca/documents/HungerCount2009NOV16.pdf>.

3 Human Resources and Skills Development Canada, "Canadians in Context – Aboriginal Population," Ottawa <http://www4.hrsdc.gc.ca/.3ndic.1t.4r@ -eng.jsp?iid=36>.

4 Food Banks Canada, *Hunger Count 2009.*

5 Dietitians of Canada, "Individual and Household Food Insecurity in Canada."

6 Ibid.

7 Ibid.

8 Ibid.

9 The Stop Community Food Centre, "Do the Math" <http://dothe-math.thestop.org/>.

10 Ottawa Public Health, "The Cost of a Nutritious Food Basket in Ottawa for 2009" <http://www.ottawa.ca/residents/health/living/nutrition/services/nfb_ 2007_en.pdf>.

11 Canada Mortgage and Housing Corporation, "Rental Market Report."

12 David McKeown, "Put Food in the Budget," *The Toronto Star*, March 18, 2009.

10: Food Insecurity: A Source of Suffering and Ill-health

1 Health Canada, Office of Nutrition Policy and Promotion, *Canadian Community Health Survey,* Cycle 2.2, *Nutrition (2004) – Income-Related Household Food Security in Canada,* 2007.

2 E. Power, Dietitians of Canada, "Individual and Household Food Insecurity in Canada: Position of Dietitians of Canada," Executive Summary, *Canadian Journal of Dietetic Practice and Research* 66 (2005):43–46 <http://www.dietitians.ca/news/downloads/Food_Insecurity_position.pdf>.

3 B. Rainville and S. Brink, *Food Insecurity in Canada, 1998–1999* (Ottawa:

Human Resources Development Canada, Applied Research Branch of Strategic Policy, 2001).

4 J. Poppendieck, *Sweet Charity? Emergency Food and the End of Entitlement* (New York: Viking, 1998).

5 Food Banks Canada, *Hunger Count 2009: A Comprehensive Report on Hunger and Food Bank Use in Canada, and Recommendations for Change*, Toronto, 2009 <www.foodbankscanada.ca>.

6 National Council of Welfare, *Welfare Incomes 2008*, Ottawa, 2010.

7 Ibid.

8 KFLA Public Health, *The Cost of Eating Healthy 2009 in Kingston*, Frontenac and Lennox & Addington, Kingston, Ont., 2010.

9 Ministry of Community and Social Services, *Special Diets Expert Review Committee: Final Report*, Toronto, 2008 <www.mcss.gov.on.ca/>.

10 Ministry of Community and Social Services, *Special Diets Expert Review Committee: Final Report*, Toronto, 2008 <www.mcss.gov.on.ca/>.

11 Kraus K. McGuinty's axing of the Special Diet Program is a catastrophe for poor and sick Ontarians <wwwrabbleca/news/2010/05/mcguintys>.

12 See 25 in 5 Network for Poverty Reduction website <www.25in5.ca>.

13 See Put Food in the Budget website <www.putfoodinthebudget.ca>.

14 D. McKeown, "Put Food in the Budget," *The Toronto Star*, March 18, 2009 <wwwthestar.com/comment/article>.

11: Poverty and Health: "I'm One Stumble from the Street"

1 H. Bosma, M.G. Marmot, H. Hemingway, A. Nicholson, E.J. Brunner, and S. Stansfeld, "Low Job Control and Risk of Coronary Heart Disease in the Whitehall II (Prospective Cohort) Study," *British Medical Journal* 314 (997):558.

2 World Health Organization, *Closing the Gap in a Generation: Health Equity through Action on the Social Determinants of Health*, Final Report of the Commission on Social Determinants of Health, November 2008 <www.who.int/social_determinants/thecommission/finalreport/en>.

3 M. Fortin, "The Connection between Low Income, Weak Labour Force Attachment and Poor Health," *Canadian Studies in Population* 37, 1–2 (2010).

4 "Canada Short Changes Mental Health Care: Kirby," *The Hook*, A Tyee Blog, June 22, 2010 <thetyee.ca/Blogs/TheHook/Health>.

5 R. Wilkinson and K. Pickett, *The Spirit Level: Why Equality Is Better for Everyone* (London: Penguin, 2009), p.20.

6 Public Health Agency of Canada, *Report on the State of Public Health 2008*, June 2008 <http://www.phac-aspc.gc.ca/publicat/2008/cpho-aspc/cpho-aspc02-eng.php#3>.

7 *The Globe and Mail*, June 17, 2010.

12: Poverty Makes Us Sick

1 D. Raphael, *Poverty and Policy in Canada: Implications for Health and Quality of Life* (Toronto: Canadian Scholars' Press, 2007).

2 D. Gordon, "The Concept and Measurement of Poverty," in *Poverty and Social Exclusion in Britain: The Millennium Survey*, ed. C. Pantazis, D. Gordon, and R. Levitas (Bristol, Eng.: The Policy Press, 2006). A rough estimate of those experiencing or close to experiencing absolute poverty in Canada is about 9 per cent of households or 2.7 million Canadians – the number reporting experiencing food insecurity in 2004. In Ontario the figure is 8.4 per cent of families or 987,600 Ontarians. See Canadian Community Health Survey, "Cycle 2.2, Nutrition (2004) – Income-Related Household Food Security in Canada" < http://www.hc-sc.gc.ca/fn-an/alt_formats/ hpfb-dgpsa/pdf/surveill/income_food_sec-sec_alim-eng.pdf.>

3 Organization for Economic Co-operation and Development, *Growing Unequal: Income Distribution and Poverty in OECD Nations* (Paris, 2008).

4 D. Raphael, "Canadian Perspectives on Poverty," in *Poverty and Policy in Canada: Implications for Health and Quality of Life*, ed. D. Raphael (Toronto: Canadian Scholars' Press, 2007).

5 D. Raphael, "Reducing Social and Health Inequalities Requires Building Social and Political Movements," *Humanity and Society* 33,1/2 (2009).

6 Human Resources and Skills Development Canada, "Work – Unionization Rates," 2010 <http://www4.hrsdc.gc.ca/.3ndic.1t.4r@-eng.jsp?iid=17>. See Jim Coyle, "Anti-Poverty Arsenal Lacks Key Weapon," *The Toronto Star*, May 7, 2008 <http://www.thestar.com/article/422233>.

7 Organization for Economic Co-operation and Development, *The Battle against Exclusion: Social Assistance in Canada and Switzerland*, 1999.

8 See "ODSP Continues to Confuse and Fail" <http://www.accessibilitynews.ca /cwdo/activities/odsp_committee.php?activities-odsp=522>.

9 See Jim Stanford, "A Reason to Celebrate: Ontario's Minimum Wage Rises to $10.25" <http://www.rabble.ca/columnists/2010/04/reason-celebrate-ontarios-minimum-wage-rises-1025>; "Coalition Celebrates Minimum Wage Passing $10 Milestone" <http://goodjobsforall.ca/?p=1041>.

10 D. Raphael, "Poverty and Health," in *Poverty and Policy in Canada*, ed. Raphael. See also "Type 2 Diabetes: Poverty, Priorities and Policy, The Social Determinants of the Incidence and Management of Type 2 Diabetes" <http://tinyurl.com/ycysb9l>.

11 D. Raphael, "The Lived Experience of Poverty," in *Poverty and Policy in Canada*, ed. Raphael.

12 F. Diderichsen, T. Evans, and M. Whitehead, "The Social Basis of Disparities in Health," in *Challenging Inequalities in Health: From Ethics to Action*, ed. T. Evans, M. Whitehead, F. Diderichsen, A. Bhuiya, and M. Wirth (New York: Oxford University Press, 2001).

13 D. Coburn, "Health and Health Care: A Political Economy Perspective," in *Staying Alive: Critical Perspectives on Health, Illness, and Health Care*, 2nd ed., ed. T. Bryant, D. Raphael, and M. Rioux (Toronto: Canadian Scholars'

Press, 2010).

14 S. Saint-Arnaud and P. Bernard, "Convergence or Resilience? A Hierarchical Cluster Analysis of the Welfare Regimes in Advanced Countries," *Current Sociology* 51,5 (2003).

15 Campaign 2000, "Family Security in Insecure Times: The Case for a Poverty Reduction Strategy for Canada, 2008 Report Card on Child and Family Poverty in Canada," Toronto, 2008; F. Baum, "Cracking the Nut of Health Equity: Top Down and Bottom Up Pressure for Action on the Social Determinants of Health," *Promotion and Education* 14,2 (2007).

16 "Social Determinants of Health: The Canadian Facts," 2010 <http://thecanadianfacts.org>.

13: Families Matter: The Catch-22 of Poverty

1 J. Lawrence Aber, Neil G. Bennett, Dalton C. Conley, and Jiali Li, "The Effects of Poverty on Child Health and Development," *Annual Review of Public Health* 18 (1997):463–83.

2 See Iowa State University, Institute for Social and Behavioral Research website, faculty and staff <http://www.isbr.iastate.edu/staff/Personals/rdconger>.

14: Ontario's Push to Early Childhood Education and Care for All

1 Petr Varmuza, oral presentation to (Ontario) Standing Committee on Social Policy. March 22, 2010.

2 Martha Friendly and Susan Prentice, *About Canada: Childcare* (Halifax: Fernwood Publishing, 2009), p.23.

3 UNICEF, *State of the World's Children Report*, 1999 <www.childcare-canada.org/res/issues/fullday1.html>.

4 See Ontario Ministry of Education website <www.ontario.ca/earlylearning>.

5 Ontario Newsroom, "Ontario Passes Full-Day Learning Act," April 27, 2010 <http://news.ontario.ca/edu/en/2010/04/ontario-passes-full-day-learning-act.html>.

15: "It's Not My Country Yet . . ."

1 Grace-Edward Galabuzi, *Canada's Economic Apartheid: The Social Exclusion of Racialized Groups in the New Century* (Toronto: Canadian Scholars' Press, 2006), p.xvii.

2 Colour of Poverty Campaign, Fact Sheet no. 1, 2007 <http://www.colourofpoverty.ca/>; Ontario Healthy Communities Coalition, "The Colour of Poverty" <http://www.ohcc-ccso.ca/en/the-colour-of-poverty>.

3 *The Toronto Star*, July 23, 2010.

4 Colour of Poverty Campaign, Fact Sheet no. 8, 2007 <http://www.colourofpoverty.ca/>.

5 Conference Board of Canada, *Making a Visible Difference: The Contribution of Visible Minorities to Canadian Economic Growth* (Ottawa, 2004).

6 Vincenzo Pietropaolo, *Not Paved with Gold: Italian-Canadian Immigrants in the 1970s* (Toronto: Between the Lines, 2006).

16: Rural Poverty: Hidden in the Country?

1 *Beyond Freefall: Halting Rural Poverty* – *Final Report of the Standing Senate Committee on Agriculture and Forestry*, Ottawa, June 2008 ⟨www.parl.gc.ca/39/2/parlbus/commbus/senate/com-e/agri-e/repo9jun08-e.pdf⟩.
2 Canadian Welfare Council, "Rural Need in Canada," Ottawa, 1965.
3 Canadian Association of Food Banks, "CAFB Responds to *Beyond Freefall: Halting Rural Poverty*, a Report of the Senate Standing Committee on Agriculture and Forestry," June 26, 2008 <www.cafb-acba.ca/documents/CAFB_Brief_Senate_Rural_Poverty.pdf>.

18: A Pebble in the Shoe

1 *The Toronto Star*, June 15, 2010.
2 A 2008 study by the Ontario Association of Food Banks revealed that poverty cost each Ontario resident $2,800 per year in additional health costs, policing, welfare, loss of human resources, mental health services related to stress, education, and child protection services. See Ontario Association of Food Banks, "The Cost of Poverty: An Analysis of the Economic Cost of Poverty in Ontario," Toronto, November 2008 <www.oafb.ca/assets/pdfs/CostofPoverty.pdf>.
3 R. Wilkinson, and K. Pickett, *The Spirit Level: Why Equality Is Better for Everyone* (London: Penguin, 2009), p.215.
4 "Incomes of the richest 10%, already the most affluent in the country, have risen rapidly in the past few years; incomes of the bottom 40% have not improved since 2000, with earlier improvements reflected in an increase in access to paid work that an expanding economy allows. Fuelling it all: a radically restructured labour market and a shrinking role for redistribution, through transfers and taxes." Armine Yalnizyan, *Ontario's Growing Gap* (Toronto: Canadian Centre for Policy Alternatives, 2007), p.5.
5 Wilkinson and Pickett, *Spirit Level*, p.230.
6 People for Education, *Private Money in Public Schools*, Toronto, August 2010; and *The Toronto Star*, Aug. 31, 2010.
7 Yalnizyan, *Ontario's Growing Gap*, p.11.
8 "The Ecological Wealth of Nations: Earth's Biocapacity as a New Framework for International Cooperation," Global Footprint Network, April 2010 <http://www.footprintnetwork.org/images/uploads/Ecological_Wealth_of_Nations.pdf>.
9 John Kenneth Galbraith, *The Culture of Contentment* (Boston: Houghton Mifflin, 1992), p.38.

Contributors

Brice Balmer is director of the Interfaith Social Assistance Reform Coalition and associate professor of practical theology at Waterloo Lutheran Seminary. For twenty-three years he was chaplaincy director at the House of Friendship, a multiservice agency serving people with low incomes in Waterloo Region.

Mira Dineen is entering her final year of study at Queen's University, where she is completing her Honours B.A. in Global Development Studies. She has organized and led workshops for elementary school students on peace education and global citizenship.

Rabbi Lawrence A. Englander has been Rabbi of Solel Congregation, Mississauga, Ontario, since its inception in 1973. He was active in founding the Mississauga Food Bank and Pathway Community Developments of Peel.

Mary Gellatly is a community legal worker in the Workers Rights Group at Parkdale Community Legal clinic. She works in partnership with the Workers' Action Centre to improve wages and working conditions for people in low-wage and precarious work.

Imam Shafiq Hudda is the spiritual leader of the Shia Muslims residing in the Waterloo-Wellington Region. During his teenage years he founded the non-profit Islamic Humanitarian Service.

Doryne Kirby is a member of the Institute of the Blessed Virgin Mary (Loretto Sisters). Doryne was the IBVM's official representative at the United Nations before returning to Toronto as Community Coordinator, Loretto College.

Elaine Power is an associate professor in the Queen's University School of Kinesiology and Health Studies. She teaches courses in the social determinants of health, health policy, and the sociology of food. She conducts research about what food means to people, especially in conditions of poverty.

Dennis Raphael is a professor of health policy and management at York University, Toronto. He is the author of *About Canada: Health and Illness* and *Poverty and Policy in Canada: Implications for Health and Quality of Life.*

Laurel Rothman is the national coordinator of Campaign 2000, a coalition of more than 120 organizations committed to poverty elimination. She has worked in the voluntary sector and for governments and the union movement in direct service, planning, policy development, and advocacy.

Bhante Saranapala is a resident Buddhist monk and meditation master at Etobicoke's West End Buddhist Cultural Centre/Monastery and a Buddhist chaplain at the University of Toronto.

Michael Shapcott is director of affordable housing and social innovation at the Wellesley Institute. A leading community-based housing expert, he has worked as a homeless outreach worker, affordable housing developer, and policy analyst.

Jamie Swift is a Kingston writer and author of numerous books on social and political issues. He is director of the Justice, Peace and Integrity of Creation Office of the Sisters of Providence of St. Vincent de Paul.

Armine Yalnizyan is senior economist with the Canadian Centre for Policy Alternatives. A lifelong activist, she has been a member of Toronto's Trinity-St. Paul United Church for three decades.